CYBERSPACE

THE WORLD OF DIGITAL ARCHITECTURE

CYBERSPACE

THE WORLD OF DIGITAL ARCHITECTURE

Published in Australia in 2001 by
The Images Publishing Group Pty Ltd
ACN 059 734 431
6 Bastow Place, Mulgrave, Victoria 3170, Australia
Telephone (61 3) 9561 5544 Facsimile (61 3) 9561 4860 .
Email: books@images.com.au
www.imagespublishing.com.au

National Library of Australia Cataloguing-in-Publication Data

Cyberspace : the world of digital architecture.

Includes index.
ISBN 1 86470 057 2.

1. Architecture - Computer-aided design.

720.28

Designed by The Graphic Image Studio Pty Ltd, Mulgrave, Australia
Film by Pageset Pty Ltd, Australia
Printed in Hong Kong

CONTENTS

INTRODUCTION

CYBERSPACE?

The term 'cyberspace', first coined by William Gibson in his 1984 science fiction novel *Neuromancer*, has today almost reached the level of common language, if not common acceptance for its place as a legitimate architectural construct. In IMAGES' latest publication, *Cyberspace—The World of Digital Architecture*, a largely visual statement of this construct is provided, thus helping advance its legitimacy even further through the featured work and words of many of its pioneers.

'Cyber', taken here to mean 'computer processed', conjoins the suffix 'space', and in doing so propagates the idea of digitally represented realms, at once both realistic and paradoxically elusive. To the observer, these realms may be perceived as tangible (real) or exotically intangible (virtual). They might, in themselves, be fluid (for example Marcos Novak's 'transarchitectures' residing or trapped within the computer medium from which they were derived) or they might be quite static, apparently realistic but realizable only with the greatest difficulty.

Whether in flux or quite still, digital landscapes, architectural environments, and even worlds, conjure up ideas of new movements—architectural, philosophical, and spatial. Of course it is the sense of spatiality that is the core ingredient of cyberspace, but how new is cyberspace in terms of its meaning?

The *Oxford English Dictionary* includes in its definition of cyberspace 'space perceived as such by an observer but generated by a computer system and having no real existence', whereas its progenitor Gibson declares it rather more lyrically to be 'A consensual hallucination experienced daily by billions of legitimate operators, in every nation, by children being taught mathematical concepts...A graphic representation of data abstracted from the banks of every computer in the human system. Unthinkable complexity. Lines of light ranged in the nonspace of the mind, clusters and constellations of data. Like city lights, receding...'. If we remove the 'computer' from Gibson's own rhetoric, his 'consensual hallucination' can be taken as having been achieved through other media prior to the digital age, not least through the written word, film, and theater.

In some ways we need to establish the credentials of cyberspace beyond the technology of its execution and communication in order to establish its legitimacy as both an intellectual and sensational stimulant. We risk undervaluing the qualities of narrative and associated arguments that predate the computer-assisted, just as we similarly risk over-privileging the technical argument espoused by its very existence. Cyberspace is more than 'for its own sake' and, as this book shows, provides fertile opportunities for representations as diverse as those of future building projects, or of ideas that might be sponsors of building form and arrangements; the spatial visualization of data, and speculations on the formal properties of ideas.

Cyberspace can therefore augment and extend the preoccupations of surrealism and subsequent situationist thinking. As Dalibor Veseley points out in his essay entitled 'Surrealism, Myth and Modernity', the primary goal of the movement was 'to reach an absolute point of reconciliation of dream and reality...'.[1] Cyberspace may already seem familiar, despite its relatively recent genesis, through our memory of film sets that predate *Neuromancer* by some decades. In fact, looking back at certain animation and title sequences, we can see a legacy of artistic and otherworldly intentions worthy of comparison with those of the latter-day hi-tech thoroughbreds.

We can also see the effectiveness of earlier uses of image, in manners similar to contemporary ones, in situations where image transcends literal exposé. Dali himself contributed to the Hollywood film industry in Hitchcock's 1945 *Spellbound*. The film included a dream sequence (severely cut upon release) featuring the slashing of an image of an eye with a giant pair of scissors. The play between the use of literal image and psychological suggestion had an impact due to its presentation on an improbable, larger-than-life scale. The nuances of this kind of representation of mental disorder now have a familiarity that otherwise predates digitally induced dream states. What then can we identify as truly innovative outcomes of incursions into cyberspace?

The pre-digital evocation of hyperrealist spaces in films such as *Spellbound* rely upon a provided narrative and an artist's (or group of artists') literal (albeit surreal in the case of *Spellbound*) interpretation. Spaces evoked in text or music may give the intellect freer rein to visualize, but we are still constrained by a more or less linear narrative. Cyber environments offer, for the first time, the potential for user interaction *within* the creative endeavor.

Video games constitute perhaps an extreme example of this, but as a singular creative voice they challenge the role of the architect far more than any previous adjunct activity such as film or theater set design. The blistering pace of development of computer power, and with it the rapidly increasing potential of both software and graphic performance, mean that in this regard the environment seems one of continual change. Compared with earlier science fiction propositions, cyberspatial predictions can be validated within a few years, necessarily implicating all of those who have access to the Internet and use it with enthusiasm. The skills required to harness the new media are extraordinary hybrids of programming ability and design sensibility.

The new skills required to generate these digital realms require different abilities from the user/participant, who is no longer in a position to play only a passive spectator's role. User-interactive movement in cyberspace, for example, involves navigation tools and navigators—avatars—who are the digital extensions or agents of the physical user, the cybernaut. This perhaps is the most important innovation within the cultural and creative environment of cyberspace, and leads to several dilemmas.

The first dilemma is the difference between print-based representations of cyberspace and fully immersive electronic environments. The second dilemma concerns the perceptions of space and time, and, as a corollary of both, movement. At its simplest, the digital realm offers the perception of space through the apparent movement of the cybernaut within a static cyberspace. As a phenomenon this is familiar, as it is no more than the electronic representation of occupation of the real world of built architecture. At its more exciting, cyberspace can be used to generate perceptions of spatial transformation occurring around the cybernaut, who of course may also be perceived as moving at the same time.

The dilemma here is one of value: producing representations of morphological changes in form and space requires a different level of skill than the more basic task of generating so-called 'flythroughs'. Should cyberspace designers produce their own algorithmic self-learning tools, such as the work of John Frazer and team ('evolutionary architecture'), or is it a perfectly reasonable proposition for the designer to rely on the algorithms that come with the various software packages? John Ruskin's view of artists needing to grind their own colors in the preparation of paint has some contemporary relevance here.

There are profound questions concerning the relationships between media, definitions of the role and skill of the cyber architect, and qualitative arguments of the value of the many and varied routes to cyber craft. These indicate that we are still in the pioneering stages. The tangible intangibility of cyberspace and all the new environments and applications being spawned from it are the most alienating factors to those most wedded to bolstering traditional definitions of architecture and the built environment. They also represent yet one more challenge to a beleaguered architectural profession, for if cyberspace becomes widely accepted within a broader definition of architecture, what is there in contemporary architectural education programs that presumes the architect to be a professional master of cyberspace?

This book, *Cyberspace—The World of Digital Architecture*, helps catalogue how far we have come in the context of still having a number of societal, artistic, craft, and educational dilemmas to resolve and develop.

Professor Mark Burry
Chair of Architecture and Building, Deakin University
July 2000

[1] Veseley, Dalibor. 'Surrealism, Myth and Modernity', *Architectural Design* (vol. 48, no. 2–3, 1978).

dECOi

AEGIS HYPO-SURFACE

This project was developed for a competition requiring an interactive artwork for the Birmingham Hippodrome theater foyer. The piece is simply a faceted metallic surface, which has the potential to physically deform in response to electronic stimuli from the environment (movement, sound, light, and so on). Driven by a bed of 3,000 pneumatic pistons, the dynamic 'terrains' will be generated as real-time calculations. The piece marks the transition from autoplastic (determinate) to alloplastic (interactive, indeterminate) space—a new species of reciprocal architecture.

1-5 The sequence of images show freeze-frame stills of the dynamic surface patterning

2

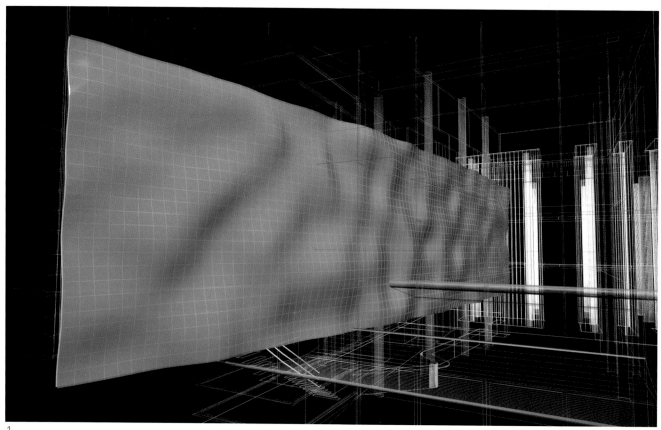

1

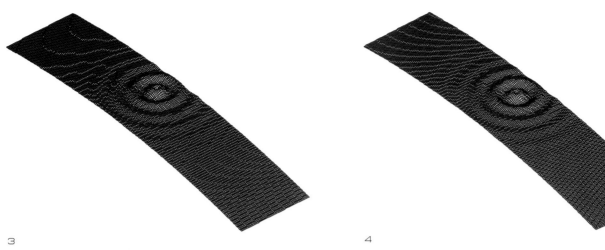

3

4

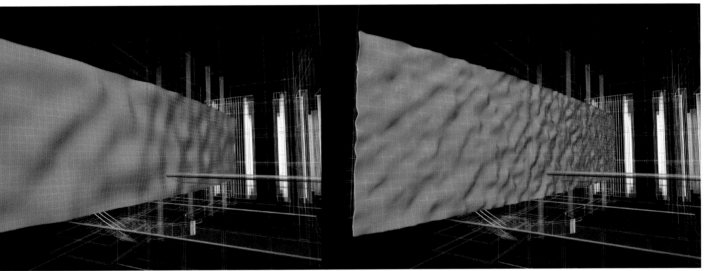

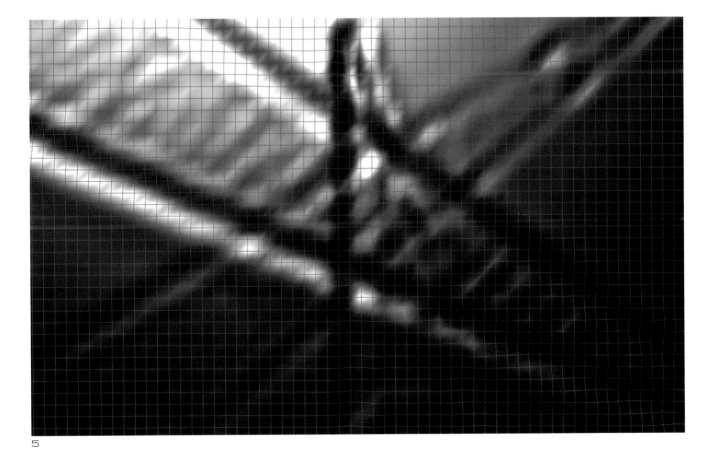

5

ARCHI-TECTONICS

AIDA HAIRSALON

Site

Aida's new hairsalon is located on the upper east side of Manhattan, and occupies a ground floor location. The design for this space is based on the idea of the wall being a smooth 'wrapper,' which starts with the facade and folds inside along the interior walls. This wrapper encapsulates all the necessities—lighting, speakers, grills, mirrors, and so on—that a hairsalon needs. The result is a soft, smooth space, where walls locally transform into desk and seating elements.

Wrapper

The facade is made of gray slate that wraps around a large glass window with a sandblasted logo, and a large pivoting frameless glass door. The transparency of the facade blurs the boundary between streetscape and interior, and invites people to walk in. A small orange light recessed in the top left corner of the stone facade replaces the traditional barber sign with an updated version.

The interior walls are all white, with frosted white plexiglass extensions for the cutting stations. Niches with suspended mirrors are backlit with orange light. At certain locations the walls fold out, reactive to program pressures; fitting rooms, pantry, and waxrooms are enveloped within.

In the back of the space, the surfaces extend into an enclosed 'green' courtyard. Benches are placed on a slate floor within groups of trees and vines, providing a cool place to wait and relax in the summer.

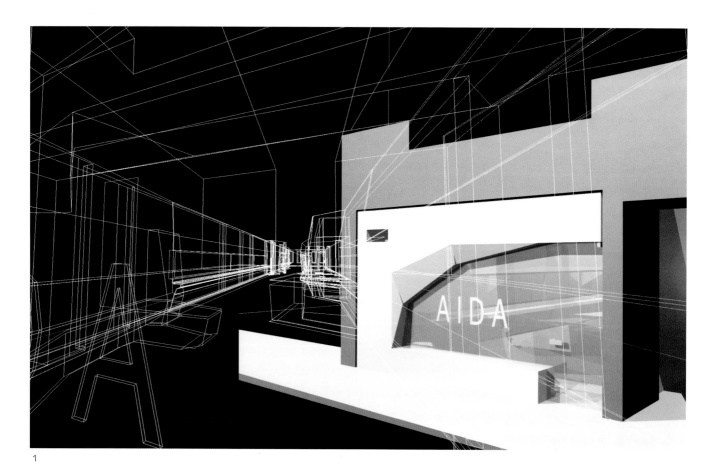

1

2

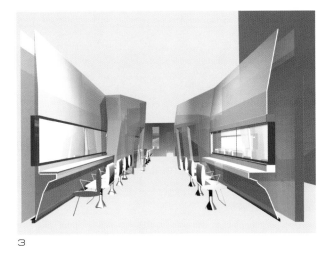

3

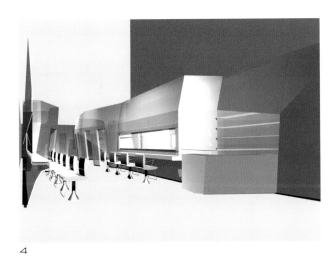

4

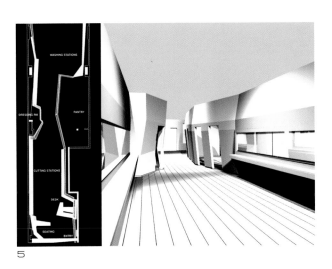

5

6

1   Facade rendering

2   View from front of salon towards garden

3   Three-dimensional section cut of wall envelope

4   Three-dimensional section cut

5   Floor plan and view of salon

6   Interior view of salon

7   Programmatic compilation and resulting wall deformations

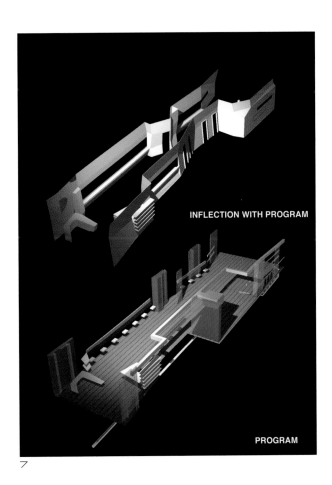

INFLECTION WITH PROGRAM

PROGRAM

7

ARCHI-**TECTONICS**

AMMAR ELOUEINI, DIGIT-ALL STUDIO

ARCHITECTURE FACULTY, UNIVERSITY OF VENICE

Acqua Alta

Venice, between the Lido, Malamocco, and Chiogga, at the meeting of the river current and the sea, identifies itself with its lagoon. Water is, at the same time, what makes it different and what would announce its loss. The core of the project plays with this ambiguity and potential.

The modification of the water surface in a fixed volumetric envelope gives rise to a new topographic space and creates tension fields, as a kind of resistance of the matter toward the constraints that are imposed on it. Movement results from this process of aspiration.

From these simulations, it is the reading of the evolution of the process over time, rather than a snapshot, that registers the deformations and their intersections.

Water, seaweed, and their movements are used as generating elements of architectural form. They generate a fluid and homogeneous architecture, where the space hierarchies, programs, and structures unroll with the fluctuations. The programmatic elements unroll in multiple crossings, streaked, like the body of a jellyfish, in a 'thick' transparency.

A chronophotographic reading of the water and seaweed aspirations creates a topographic architecture of layers (horizontal and vertical) in which the programmed spaces and the empty ones interpenetrate to form a fluid and homogeneous unit.

The program unrolls between the constitutive layers resulting from the movement of seaweed according to several criteria:

- transparency—from the lagoon to Cadoros in a movement of the ground in relation to the auditorium and restaurant.

- proximity of water—coffee, restoration, and interior channel of lifting.

- widening—in the north of the building to accommodate the offices and conference rooms of the architecture school.

- evolution—the interstitial and lamellar definition of space does not fix the positioning of all the programmatic elements.

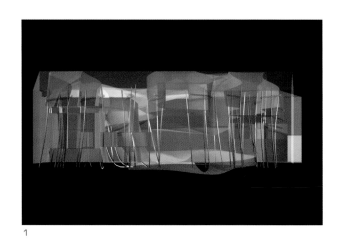

1

1 Section through building showing interior spaces
2 Phases of design process
3 View from canal looking at auditorium and restaurant
4 At the entrance under the auditorium
5 View from docks

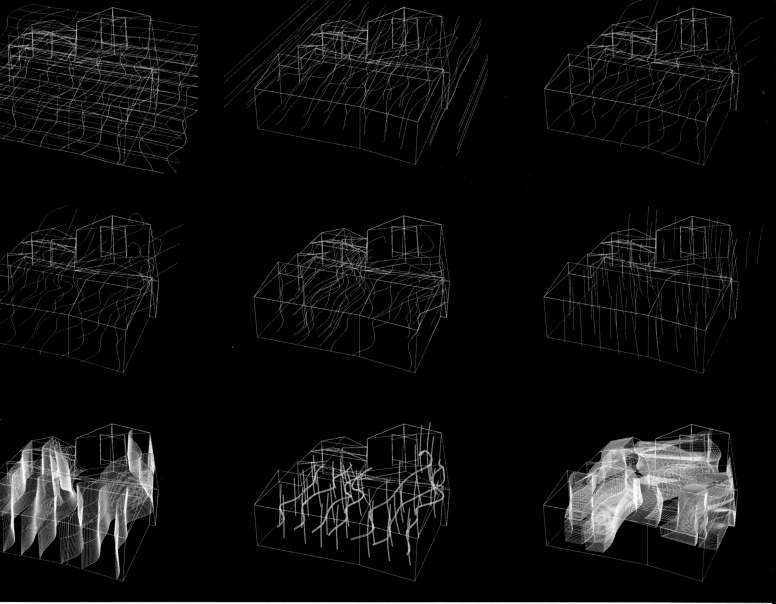

2

3

4

5

AMMAR ELOUEINI, **DIGIT-ALL STUDIO**

UN STUDIO
VAN BERKEL & BOS

The Architecture Faculty building and site form a continuous surface that fluently links the new program and the quayside, guiding public circulation. At ground level, the linear form of the quay turns into a hollow core at the centre of the volume, and rises up to form an elliptical pipe, which spills over into the roof volume at the top, organizing the distribution of the program from within.

Orienting the Surface

The proposal is derived from interpretations of characteristic Venetian architectural and urban conditions. Firstly, in keeping with the notion of Venice as a continuous, water-bound plateau incorporating routes, squares, and buildings, the maritime zone is seen as a continuous surface that links the new building and the quayside. The basic coherence of the plateau has kept the city together throughout historic change; contemporary additions have merged into the existing fabric effortlessly. Secondly, the proposal takes up the notion of the absence of an end perspective by basing its distribution system on an elliptical core, entailing the repeated turning of corners. Thirdly, the proposal's strong center is based on the organizational typology of the traditional Venetian palace, in which the great salon is the route to all other spaces and as such is the most public of the private rooms.

The ground level is kept open—the building only touches the ground in two irregular 'footprints'. The entrance at the inside of the larger footprint gives access to the stepped slope of the elliptical core. The second floor contains the large auditorium, with 500 seats and 12 lecture halls. The lecture halls are reached by means of tubular corridors projecting from the elliptical core. The top level mixes private and public functions.

The upper volume has a layered facade, creating a cohesive appearance for the volume as a result of the same components being used throughout, even in the internal walls and on the roof terrace. At the same time, subtle differentiation emerges through variations in the composition of the package. The facade system consists of a structural layer of steel beams, followed by a layer of three different types of perforated, prefabricated concrete panels. The three panel types are gridded with a cylindrical motif, introducing a modern variation on Venetian windowpanes. Finally, a steel mesh covers most of the facades, reflecting the water and rendering the facade more or less transparent.

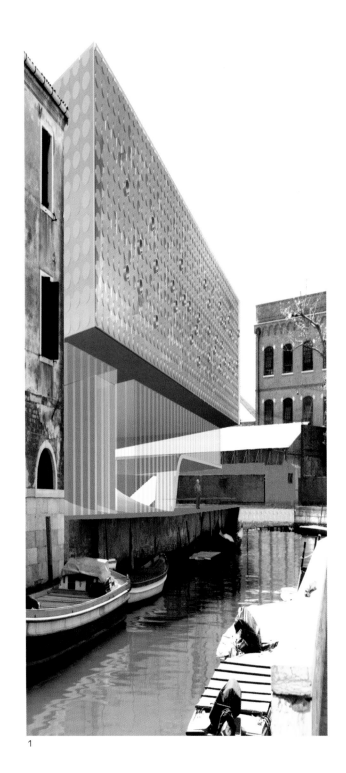

1

1 Situation of project on the site
2 General structure with circulations
3 Central court

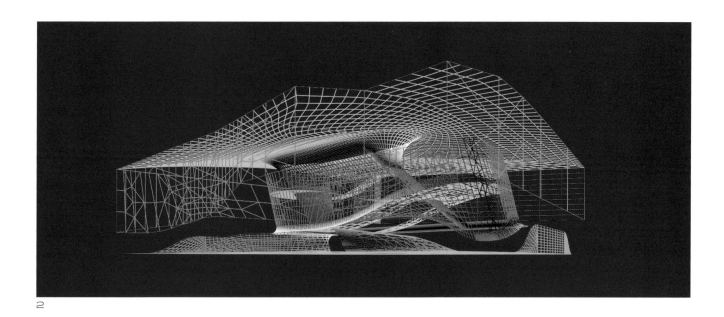

2

3

UN STUDIO **VAN BERKEL & BOS**

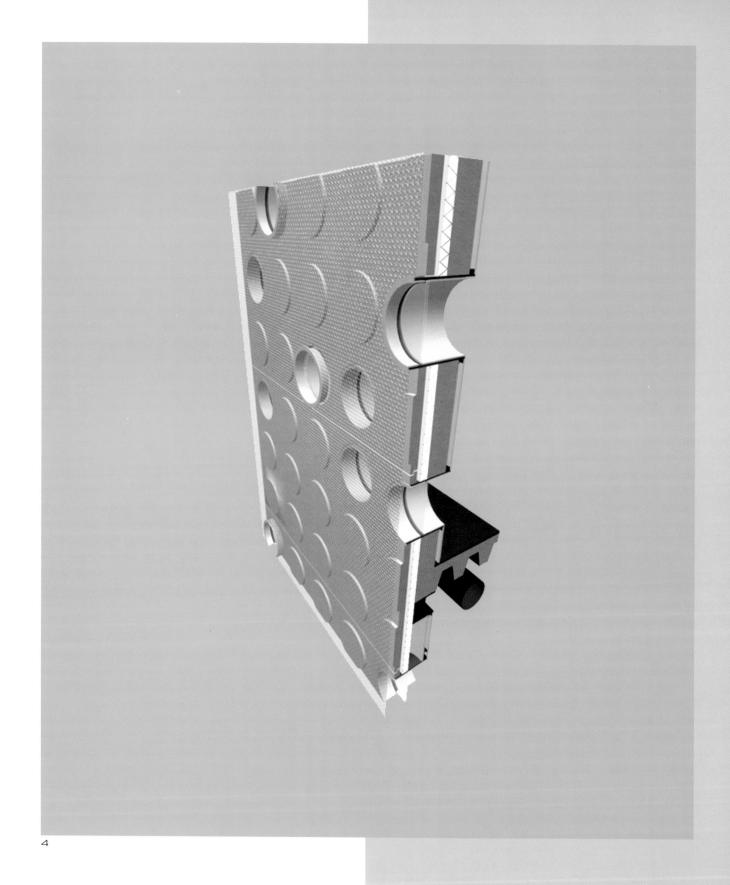

4

4 Facade detail
5 Inner court
6 Lecture room

5

6

GRANT DUNLOP & MARK BURRY

THE BOOLEAN HOUSE

Boolean Modeling Speculations

This project explores the generation of a theoretical house for George Boole (1815–1864) using logical operations named after him. The 'sculpting' procedures in most modeling software packages share the same philosophical approach to thought and logic implicit within Boolean operations. Such an approach sponsors a critical position with regard to the dominance of form over space and spatial experience influencing much of contemporary architecture. The carving and sculpting possibilities offered by software that includes Boolean modeling offer a carving out of space within an otherwise arbitrary architectural solid resulting in an almost primordial generation of the interior space: the Boolean house.

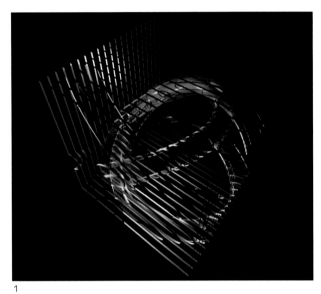

1

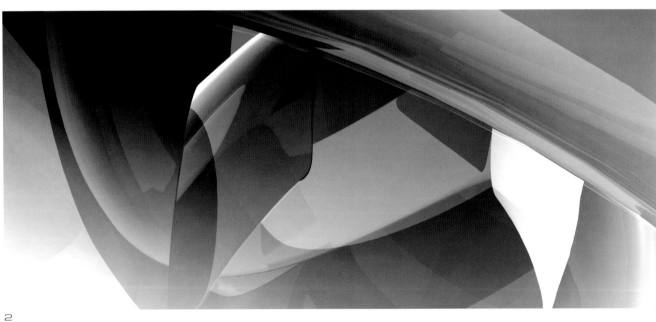

2

1   Section through the resultant form

2   View up through internal void

3-5   Boolean operations; generic volume with subtracted, additive and intersected forms

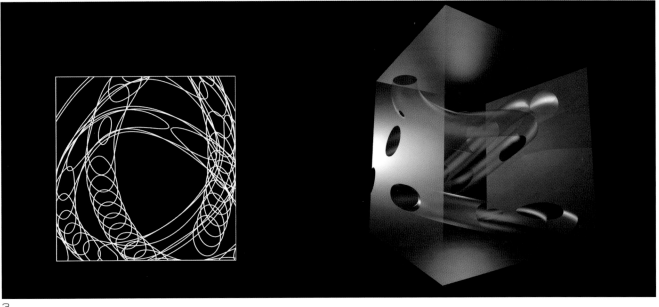

3

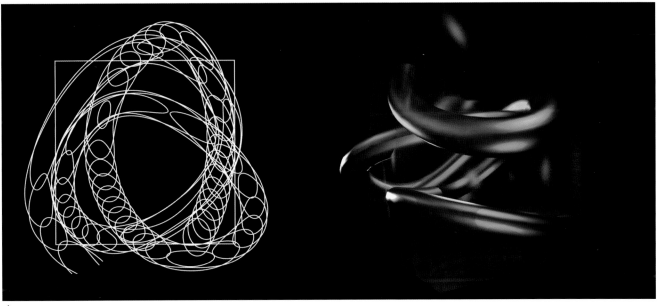

4

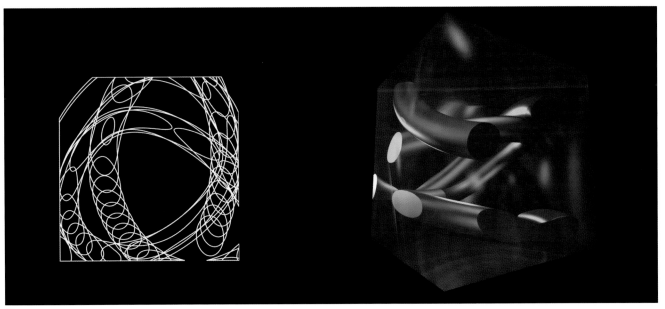

5

GRANT DUNLOP **& MARK BURRY**

CHRISTOPHER ROMERO
OSCILLATION/STUDIO 313

THE CAPTOR

The Captor was created as part of an ongoing exhibition called The Second World Exhibition, curated by Alternet Fabric and Canal+ in Lausanne, Switzerland and Paris, France. A small group of architects, designers, and artists were invited to 'install' work in a virtual museum space, creating a combined extendable environment on the shared network of the Internet. Each of the participants was given specific guidelines for building the shared environment in VRML in order to put in place a controlled organizational structure for accessing, navigating, experiencing, and exiting the work.

The Captor is a living digital system that has an existence without the presence of the 'museum' visitor. In other words, the space has behavioral characteristics that do not rely on a visitor's input or navigation. For the visitor, the experience is abrupt, disorienting, chaotic, and frightening. The system is in control of the visitor and one finds it almost impossible to gain any sense of control to exit the environment. The Captor is a controlling, progressive, computational system. It is a project that illustrates the idea of losing control of 'enabling' technologies.

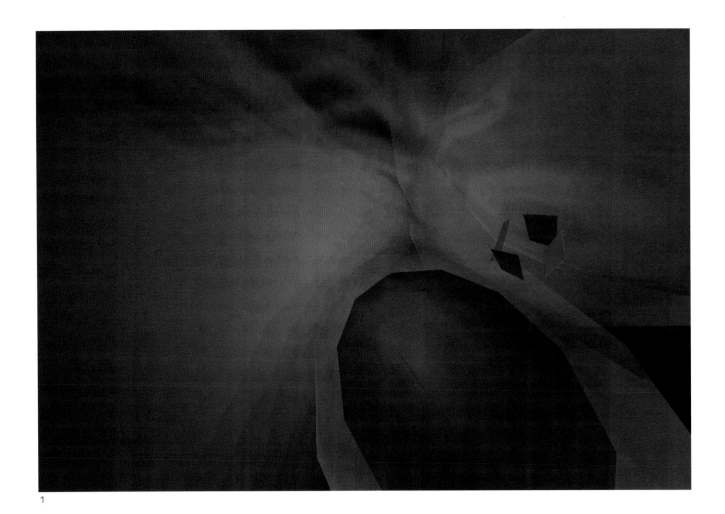

1

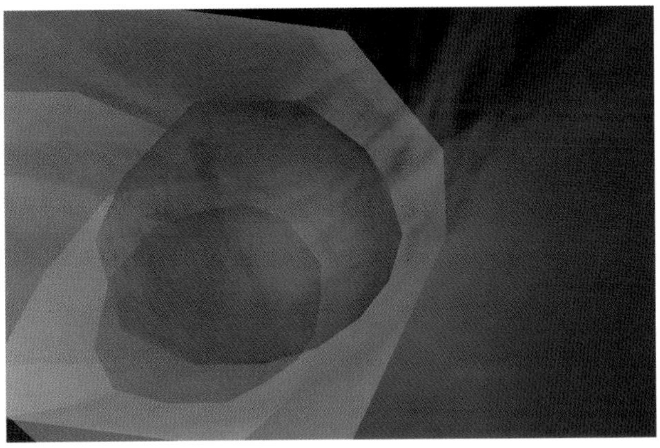

2

3

4

5

6

7

CHRISTOPHER ROMERO **OSCILLATION/STUDIO 313**

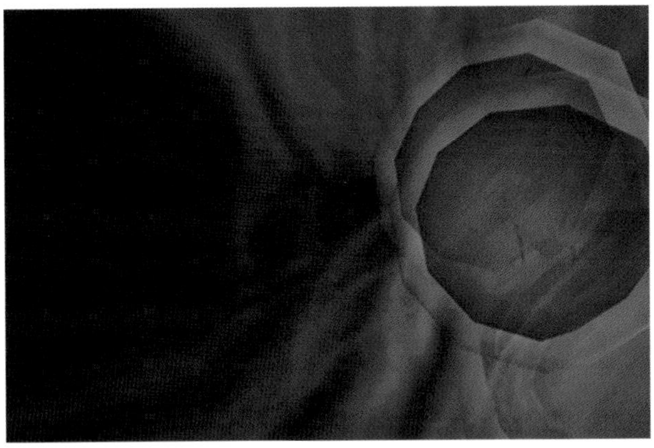

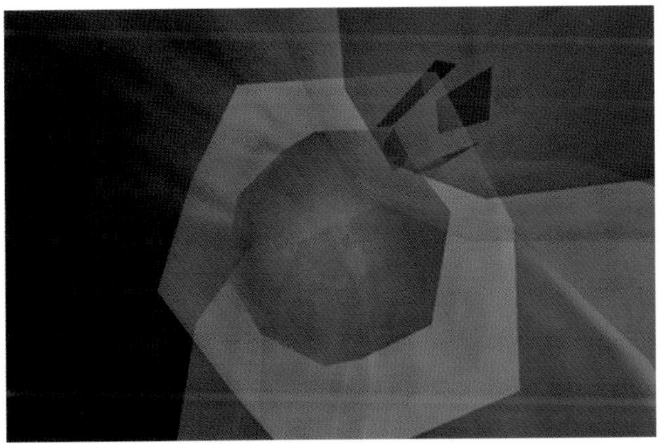

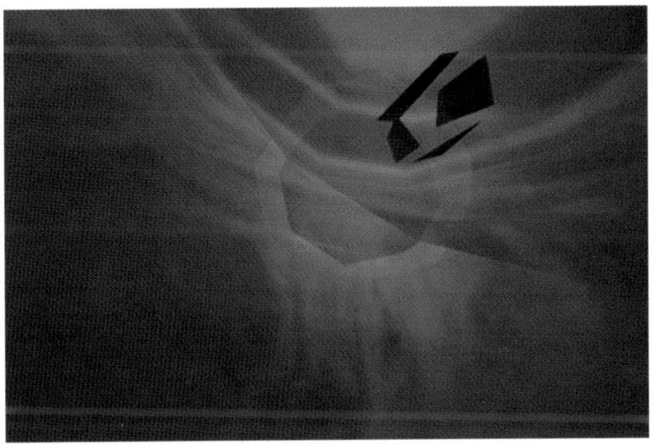

CHIMERICAL HOUSINGS: MASS CUSTOMIZED HOUSING

Chimerical Housings constitutes the initial portion of a long-term project that focuses on experimental designs for mass-customized, prefabricated housing. Shown here is one example of a sampling set of five houses. These five houses were selected from a series of digitally designed variants. All variants originate from the same 'genetic pool'. Information for the genetic pool was generated from a normative three-bedroom, two-and-a half-bathroom colonial house plan as 'base', and a range of object-products as 'targets'. Subsequent digital blending operations between the base and a varying number of targets in turn produced a large range of 'chimerical' housings.

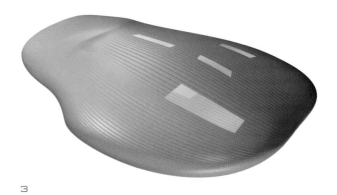

3

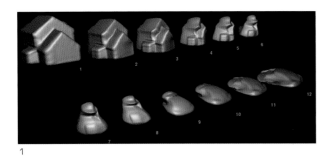

1

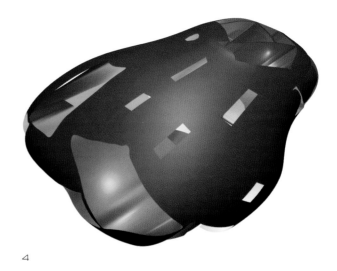

4

4

3

2

1

2

5

6

7

1 First line of transforming

2 Second line of transforming

3 Bungalow housing; exterior view

4 Bungalow housing; interior view

5&7 Golf course housing; interior view

6 Golf course housing; exterior view

KOLATAN/MAC DONALD **STUDIO**

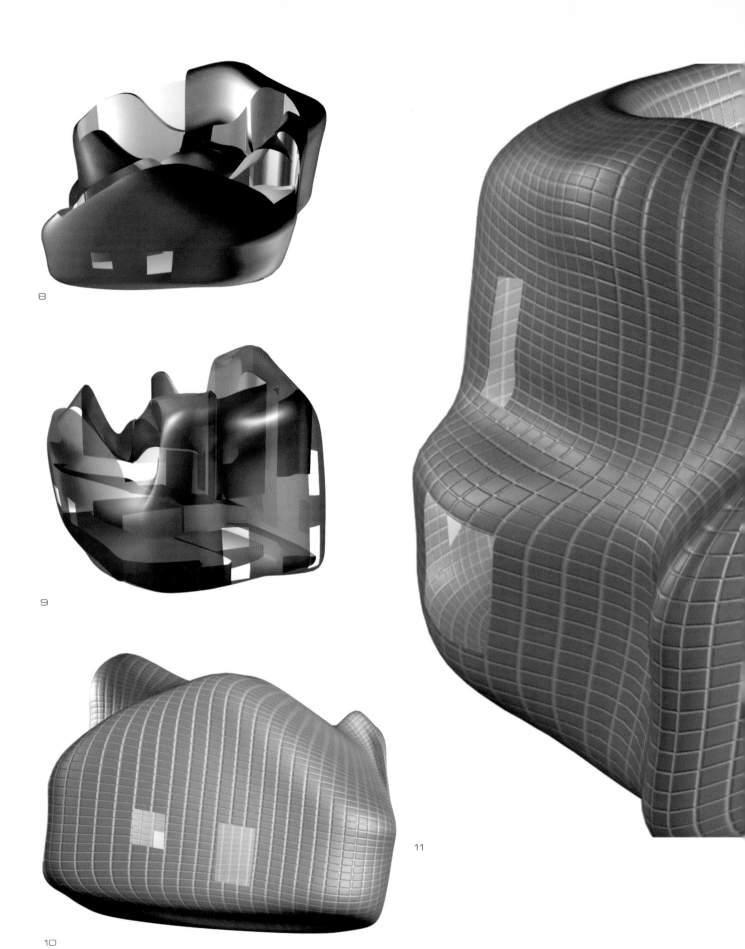

8

9

10

11

CYBER**SPACE**

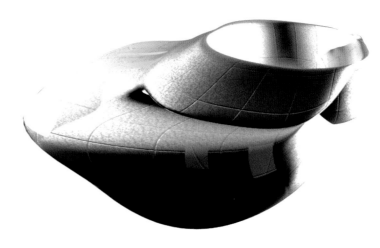

12

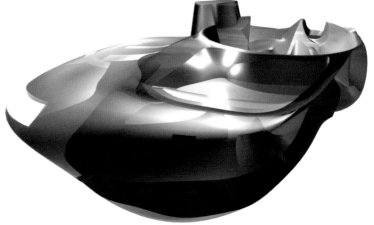

13

14

KOLATAN/MAC DONALD **STUDIO**

15&18   Shingle housing; interior view
16&17   Shingle housing; exterior view

15

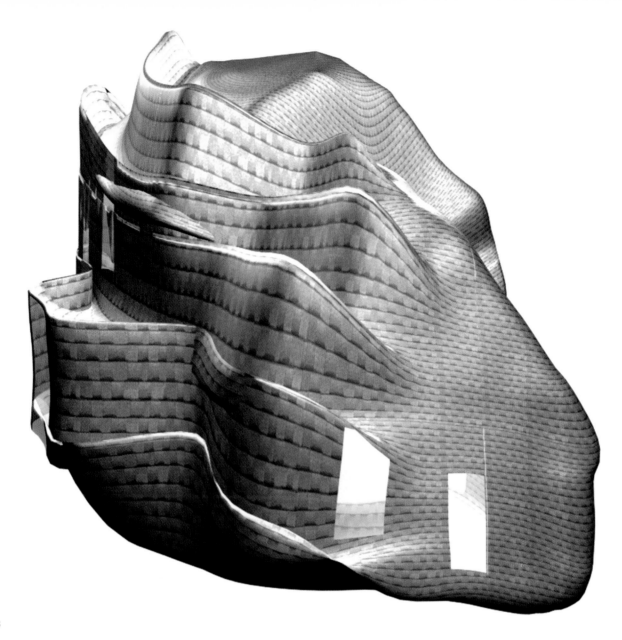

16

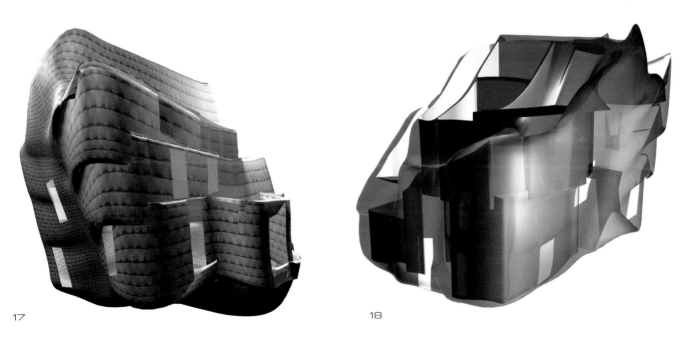

17   18

KOLATAN/MAC DONALD **STUDIO**

HARIRI & HARIRI

THE CINE EXPERIMENTAL FILM CENTER

The Experimental Film Center is a complex located on a pier near the base of the Brooklyn Bridge in New York, and is envisioned to be completed in the year 2020. The complex explores both the relationship of architecture and film through its form and structure, and the nature of entertainment in the new millennium.

With the new digital technology already changing the process of photography through digital cameras, and the abundance of new digital video technology being introduced to the entertainment and communication markets, one can only imagine how film and the movie industry will change in the near future.

The screens in the Center can be seen from the street or the river, and are made using digital micromirror device (DMD) technology. These screens can be programmed to display information, receive and show films via satellite, and can be used as a screen on which to project movies. Virtual actors and virtual sets and locations are all stored within the Center and can be reconfigured into a new movie at any time.

The complex is a pier structure with a series of structural concrete frames holding different parts of its program. A digital screen on the Brooklyn side gives a preview of the films showing and marks the entrance to the film school and the complex. The school structure is a rectangular box containing classrooms, screening and editing rooms, and sound studios, offering state-of-the-art technology and equipment for filmmaking.

1

CYBER**SPACE**

1 Overall view
2 Site plan

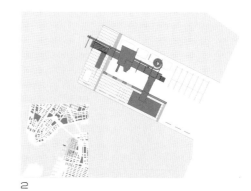

HARIRI**&HARIRI**

3

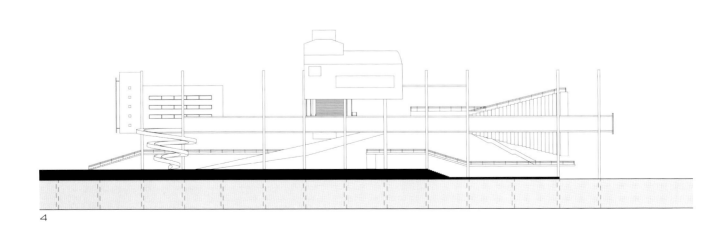

4

5

The film track gallery is a long tube accessed by a spiral ramp from the street and open to the public. The gallery exhibits film strips on its DMD windows, so that the film strip on exhibit can be viewed from both inside and from the benches on the plaza outside.

In the center of the structure, three theaters with vertical and horizontal digital screens challenge the common screen dimensions and possibilities by changing the format of new movies. At the end of the pier is a large indoor/outdoor theater for film festivals, bringing together the next generation of filmmakers.

6

7

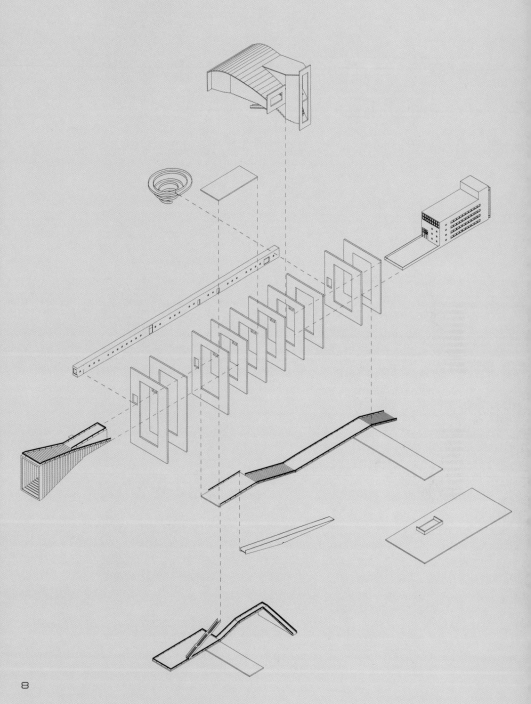

8

6 Outdoor cinemas and exhibition gallery
7 Shooting deck
8 Exploded isometric

Hyperspace Architecture

The quantum increase in information, knowledge, and technology, and the resulting complexity of human experience, have led to the hyperculture in which we are now living. In the design of architectural spaces and structures, this 'hyperization' is mirrored by the visual and spatial complexity of hyperspace architecture based on higher-dimensional geometries (hypergeometries). Hyperspace architecture can be expediently visualized in cyberspace, and can also be built as physical environments, albeit after projection into three dimensions. Cloud Cover and Spheroids (see pages 162–5) are two architectonic studies based on ongoing work by this designer over the past two decades in the application of hypergeometry to architecture. The studies are context-free and can be adapted to be site- and program-specific.

Cloud Cover

Cloud Cover hovers over an open space suitable for art and industry exhibits, performances, and temporary events. This irregular but modular hypersurface covers a space of modest size. It is constructed from identical connectors and a few types of light-sensitive panels, and can be assembled and reassembled in a variety of configurations to suit layouts on one or more levels. The irregular geometry produces a constantly varying transparency as one walks through the space. The structure is projected from 27 dimensions and will most likely require stabilizing devices.

1

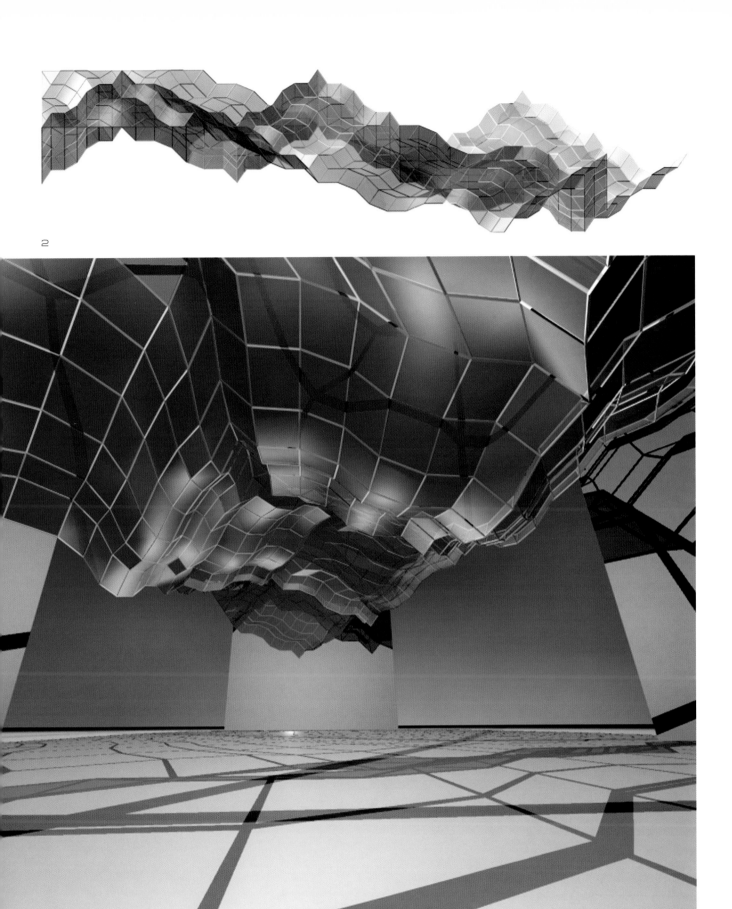

2

3

1 Exterior view
2 Elevation view, roof surface only
3 Interior view

DR HARESH **LALVANI**

Meta-Architecture

Architecture based on morphological coding of structures, in combination with computer-aided manufacturing, provides a new paradigm for the making of architectural spaces, structures, and envelopes. This approach integrates advances in spatial and structural morphology with advances in building technologies, and permits an endless production of software-driven architecture. This modeling draws from an integrated, open-ended, higher-dimensional morphological universe, and is ideally suited for exploration in cyberspace.

The author has been modeling and encoding this hyperuniverse over the last two decades. The concept provides a way to model nature's designs as well as new designs not found in nature, and opens up the possibility for the emergence of a new field of 'architectural genetics'.

The design and fabrication of curved waveforms from sheet materials (for example, metals, plastics, fiber-boards, and so on) provide an interesting application for this concept. An experiment in sheet metal with Milgo/Bufkin, New York, provided an opportunity to test the concept in one material (metal) for one industry (building). Column Museum and Waveknot (see pages 200–1) are two spin-off architectonic studies based on this experiment.

Column Museum

Column Museum is part of the universe of all possible architectural columns (past, present, and future). It displays algorithmically derived, wavy columnar structures, many of which have been prototyped in metal by Milgo/Bufkin.

The museum can be visualized as a physical installation on a suitable site, or can be seen as a virtual museum through which a viewer can navigate via a chosen pathway in cyberspace.

The virtual museum is a museum without walls and without an entrance or exit. Any point within the virtual space is an entrance or exit, so that visitors can choose their own pathway within the universe and 'enter' the museum from any point located in it.

The museum is open-ended, as new columns can be continually added to increase the repertoire. Similar museums are possible for other architectural elements and morphologies, and all are linked in the morphological hyperuniverse, a meta-universe for all architecture.

1

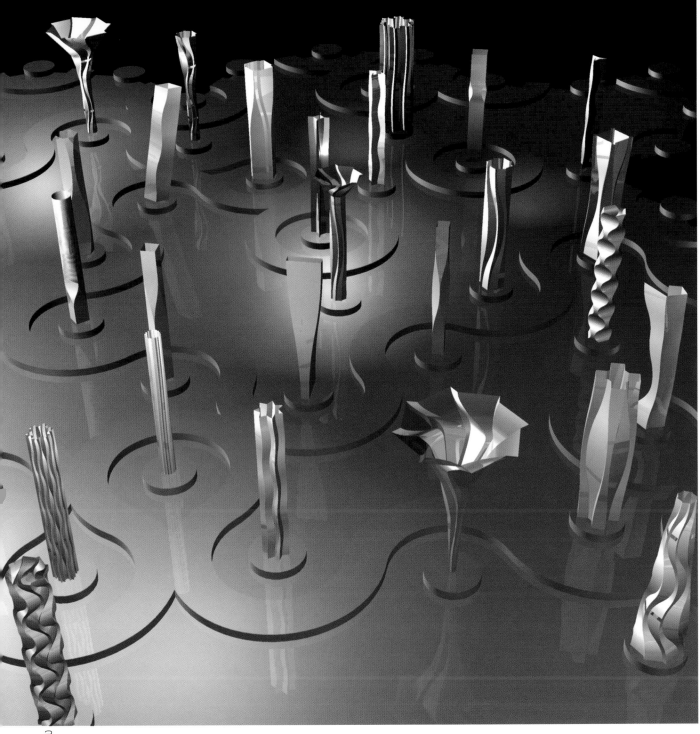

1 Close-up, perspective view

2 Aerial view

3 Elevation view in perspective

DR HARESH **LALVANI**

AMMAR ELOUEINI, DIGIT-ALL STUDIO

CULTURAL INFORMATION EXCHANGE CENTER

Located at the eastern end of Wall Street, the Cultural Information Exchange Center was designed to be a temporary structure. The small scale of the site, in comparison to the large neighboring sites, brought up the challenge of designing a small structure that could hold up against the monumental scale of surrounding buildings. Temporariness was understood as a way to generate architectural form.

Capture

The elaboration of a conceptual process started as an attempt to create a new architectural space, without getting involved in the early stages of design and without any reference to a building's typology, or architectural repertoire of form. The space was considered as an ether, and the design intention was to capture a space rather than imposing one. To accomplish this goal, the process of design started with computer simulations, using 'flock animation'.

Ether

The building is considered as a flow of bodies and information through space, over time. The programmatic elements are modeled as attractors on the site. Visitors, information, and exchanges are modeled as particles. Once the particles attract, they start to form varying degrees of concentration. A halo of particles floats over the site, suggesting an eventual architectural space. As a cloud in the sky, the particle halo starts forming a virtual building, a constellation of interrelated spatial fields. This constellation is then crystallized to form the new temporary Cultural Information Exchange Center.

1 Sequence of frames showing use of Meta-Clay System to model pedestrian flow
2 Structure of the building from Wall Street
3 Phases of design process

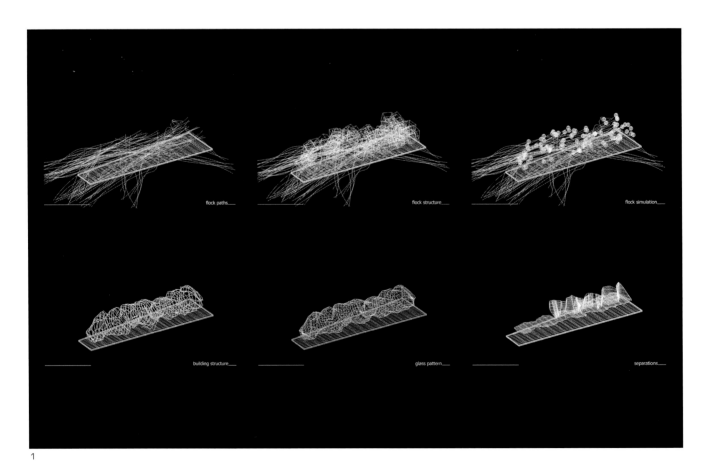

1

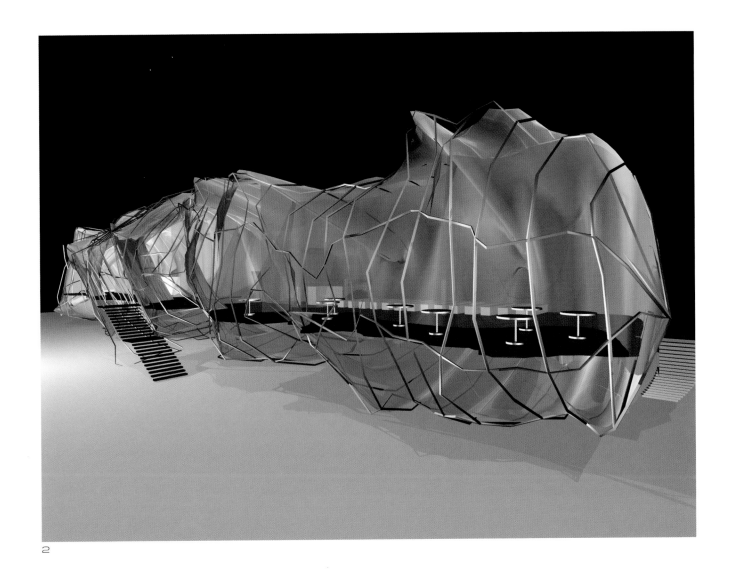

2

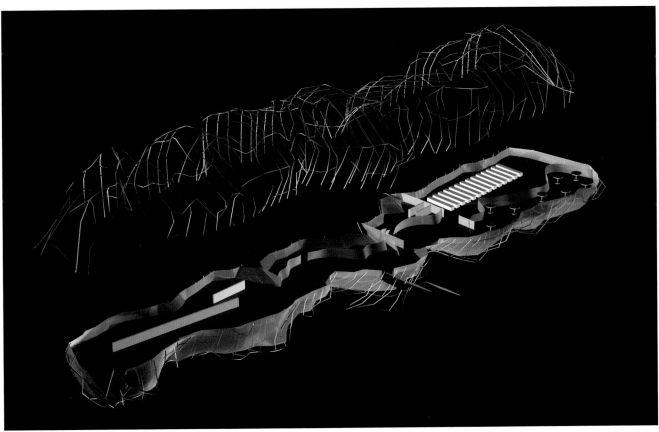

3

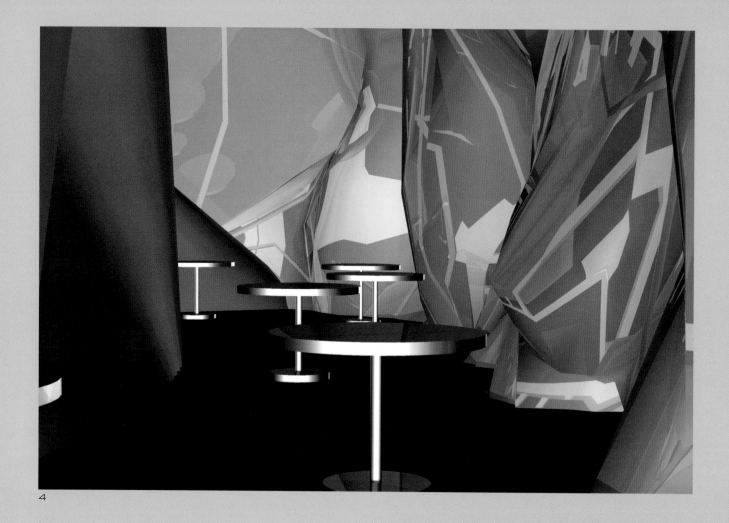

4

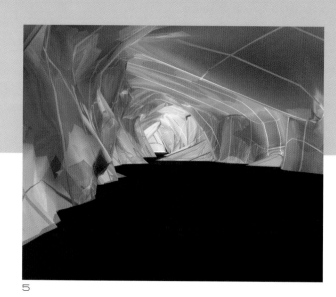

5

4 Axonometric view, showing different
  programmatic elements

5 Interior view of main exhibition space

6 View from Wall Street

7 Section through entrance, showing
  interior divisions of space

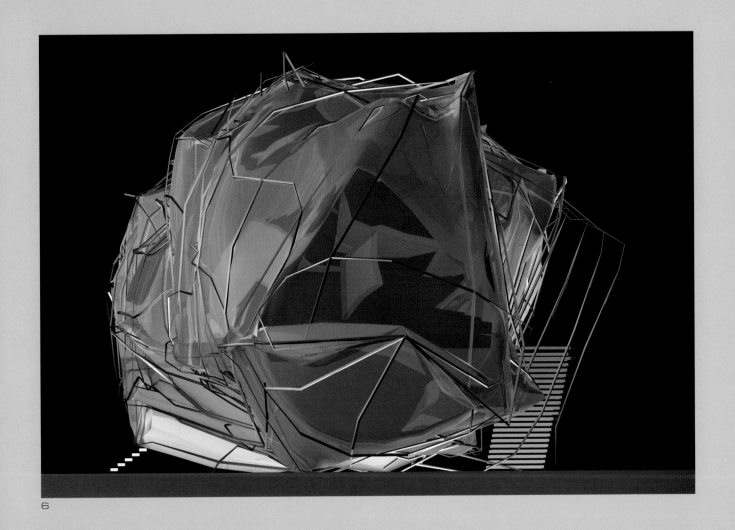

6

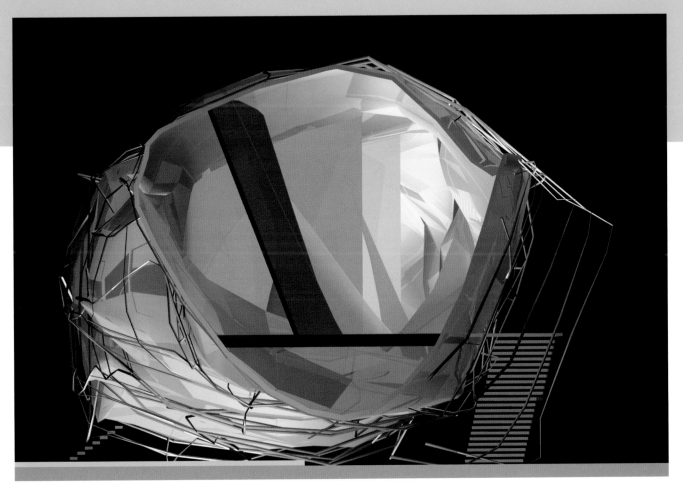

7

AMMAR ELOUEINI, **DIGIT-ALL STUDIO**

ARQUITECTONICA

CYBERPORT

Design Intent

Cyberport is a series of interconnected structures, built on reclaimed land, that zigzags along the coastline, affording all spaces in the complex a view of the water. An internal 'IT (information technology) street'—a horizontal space running from one end of the complex to the other, from the residential area and hotel through the entire office complex—interconnects all spaces. The 'IT street' connects to combinations of technical and recreational spaces, mixing together training and meeting rooms, multimedia laboratories, a cyber library, web television studios, fitness center, cafes, lounges, and bars. The design allows employees and companies to interact in both business and recreational ways, mixing employees from the larger, established firms with those from the smallest of the cutting-edge start-ups, and providing interaction that should be mutually beneficial. Office spaces throughout the complex are totally flexible and can be arranged and rearranged, both horizontally and vertically,

to accommodate the needs and growth of all types of firms. The design also includes a Cyber Center with retail and entertainment facilities, and a garden terrace overlooking a lake.

Project Description

Cyberport is a major infrastructure project being developed by Pacific Century Group, working in a partnership with the government of Hong Kong to attract IT business to that city. The site is a 64-acre parcel of virgin land on which will be built a new Silicon Valley. This 'high-tech' office and residential campus will be built at Telegraph Bay and will be opened in phases over a period of four to five years, beginning in early 2002. All images are courtesy of the Government of Hong Kong Special Administrative Region.

1

1 East elevation of office buildings with cascading terraces overlooking lake
2 View from hill of office structures
3 Aerial view of office tower, plaza and connecting office buildings

2

3

4

5

6

4 View of 'IT' Street that connects interiors of buildings

5 Interior perspective of Cyber Bar

6 Office tower lobby; *Bauhinia Blakeana*, city flower of Hong Kong, used throughout as symbolic reminder of balance between nature and technology

7 Interior perspective of Cyber Library

7

DIGITAL DESIGN PROCESS, ARCH 135

The images presented here are from Arch 135, University of California Berkeley, taught by lecturer John Marx, AIA. This is a course that studies a comprehensive process of architectural design using three-dimensional computer modeling programs, and two-dimensional computer graphics programs. The objective in the first half of the course is to gain an understanding of an alternative design methodology, which augments traditional architectural practices. The vehicle for this study is the design of a simple building, created exclusively by means of a computer. The process extends from massing models to detailed finished models, wherein every mullion and texture may be modeled. The completed three-dimensional building design is used to study two-dimensional forms of representation and creative expression.

The second half of the course studies the use of two-dimensional computer graphics as a medium for creative expression. The goal is to explore digital presentation as a creator of meaning that goes far beyond the traditional use of plan, elevation, or perspective. Computer graphics offers new opportunities to express process as an element of a presentation, as well as the ability to create great depth in layered meaning, which would have been inordinately time-consuming to do using traditional techniques. The final project is a poster that expresses the essence of the architectural design concept.

1

2

CYBER**SPACE**

3

4

1&3 Elisa Lui
  2 Jerry Jai
  4 Wilson Au-Yeung

5

6

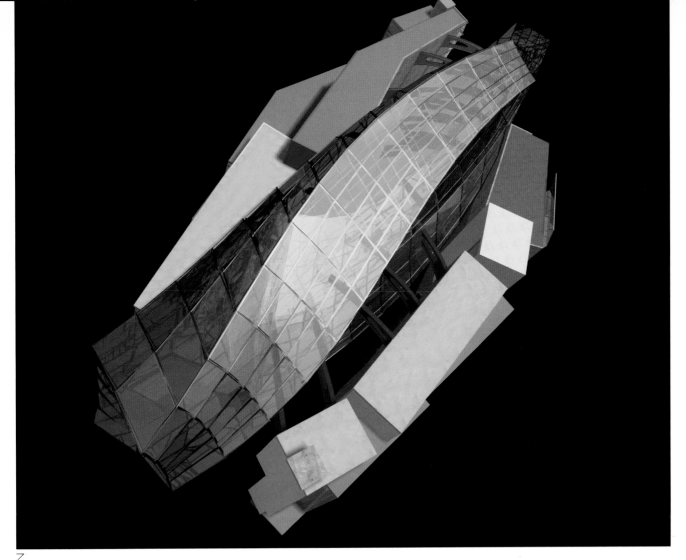

7

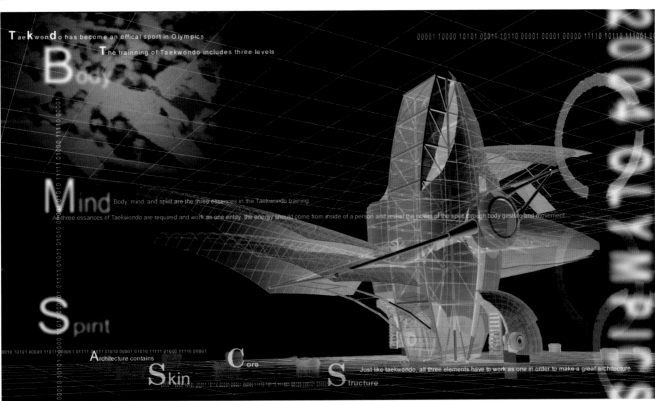

Taekwondo has become an offical sport in Olympics.
The trainning of Taekwondo includes three levels

Body

Mind Body, mind, and spirit are the three essences in the Taekwondo training.
All three essances of Taekwondo are required and work as one entity, the energy should come from inside of a person and reveal the power of the spirit through body gesture and movement.

Spirit

Architecture contains Core
Skin Structure Just like taekwondo, all three elements have to work as one in order to make a great architecture.

8

HARIRI & HARIRI

THE DIGITAL HOUSE

This project explores the nature of domestic space in the new millennium by examining the family structure, our changing habits, the institution of marriage, children, single-sex families, communication and information technologies, work, leisure, public and private life, and conceptions of body, health, and hygiene.

We believe that the physical form of a typical home has to change to reflect the apparent changes in the family structure. The programmatic and spatial requirements of the home have yet to reflect the rapid evolution of life at the closing of the industrial century. Due to the advent of new digital technology and global telecommunications, the architecture of the new millennium will have to accommodate working, shopping, schooling, entertainment, and physical fitness, all of which will take place at home. The Digital House is devised as a prototype for examining architecture in the new millennium.

The house is organized around a touch-activated digital spine, which has a steel structure and a glass enclosure made of active matrix liquid crystal displays (AMLCDs)—the building block of the new millennium. (AMLCDs combine microelectronics and amorphous materials technologies to construct transparent, thin-film transistors on an active plate. These high-definition, flat-panel displays are now being used in military aircraft as well as NASA's space shuttle fleet.)

In the Digital House, the architecture of the main spaces has been reduced to simple, efficient, and minimal habitable units, partially prefabricated and available off the shelf. These units plug into the steel structure of the spine, similar to an industrial shelving unit. In contrast to the three prefabricated volumes for sleeping (bedrooms), working (office and school), and virtually simulated common entertainment (living/dining, kitchen) plugged into the digital spine, are the transient spaces (circulation) for the inhabitants to unplug themselves momentarily, moving between tasks from the virtual to the actual world, contemplating their physical fitness and spiritual wellbeing.

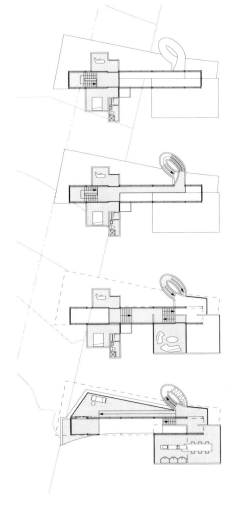

1

1 Plans
2 Elevation with actual and virtual imagery
3 Driveway, carport and plugged-in volumes
4 Exploded isometric; steel structure and
   pre-fabricated units

2

3

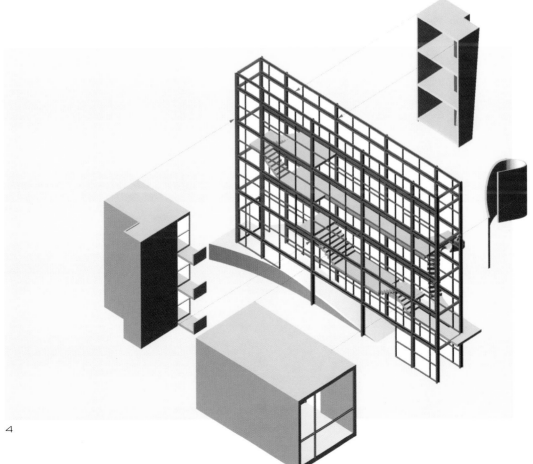

4

HARIRI **&** HARIRI

5

5 Back view
6 Entry with virtual visitors
7 Living and dining with virtual guest
8 Office with liquid drafting wall

The Digital House is for a family of three independent beings, free from preconceived notions of gender roles, domination, and sexual preference. The architecture of this house allows the family members to interact virtually but live together actually, addressing the paradoxical American desire for a solitary existence and family interaction at the same time.

The site is a two-acre suburban lot, slightly sloped towards an artificial lake. The actual landscaping around the house is a typical low-maintenance lawn with trees marking the lot lines. The virtual landscaping, however, can offer many possibilities throughout the house.

All bedrooms are equipped with a dream-recording device, so one can review one's dreams on the liquid wall of the room at any time. The office/work spaces have liquid drafting walls replacing today's individual computer monitors; consequently the children's work/classrooms are connected to schools around the globe.

The kitchen/dining area operates like a laboratory, with a long working counter also plugged into the spine. One can prepare a meal with the help of a virtual chef from a favorite restaurant and have dinner with a virtual guest or friend through the liquid wall. The living room on the upper part is where the entertainment takes place (media room). Any movie or television program is accessible globally and can be watched from a soft, organic, and comfortable sofa.

6

7

8

9

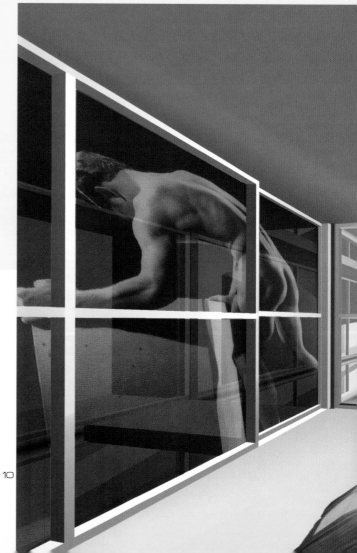

10

CYBER**SPACE**

11

9 Entry hall– transient space with ramp

10 Bedroom with dream recording device

11 Kitchen with virtual chef

ARCHI-TECTONICS

DIS-A-PIER FLUID TOPOLOGIES

Site

The City of Yokohama has designated the artificially reclaimed land along the harbor as a large new corporate entity for the city, a 'dynamic urban development'. It consists of two areas. Minato Mirai 21, a new zone close to the pier, primarily comprises high-rises and large business enterprises. This typifies the notion of corporate power—the static, stable part of society. The Osanbashi pier, the future site for the port terminal in the city, forms a space of movement, a dynamic, temporal space, a space of arrival and departure. The visitor experiences delay, the momentary stretching of time.

Concept

The notion of delay is introduced through a topological model in which two 'twisted rubber bands' distill this time lapse within the space of the terminal. The two twisted surfaces are loaded with program, one the carrier of city functions, the other of terminal functions. The intersection of the two bands results in a series of functional modules, which simultaneously smoothly connect with and slip past each other.

Terminal Functions

The terminal, containing the departure/arrival hall and Customs, Immigration, and Quarantine area (CIQ), is located in the tightly intertwined space formed by the intersection of two topological bands, which produces a 'bridge' structure. This allows a traffic plaza to be located under the terminal, where visitors can wander around the pier freely, and where the entrance of the departure/arrival hall is located. After checking in, passengers cross the traffic plaza to the CIQ, where luggage is checked in, and then depart via the cruise decks. Visitors can accompany passengers over the bridge and ascend to the

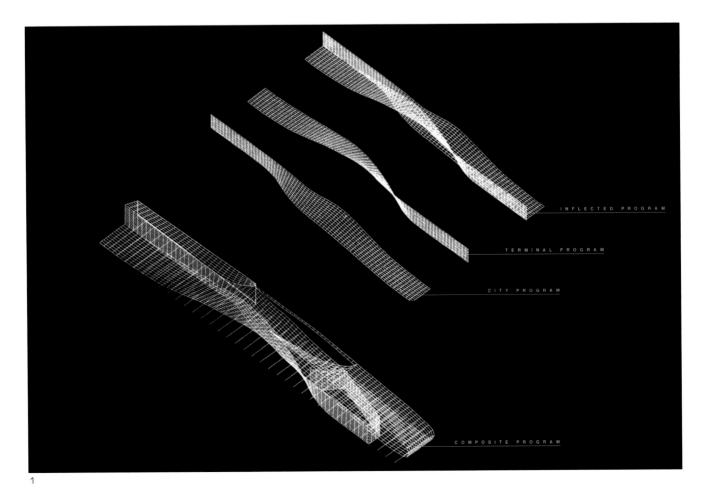

INFLECTED PROGRAM

TERMINAL PROGRAM

CITY PROGRAM

COMPOSITE PROGRAM

1

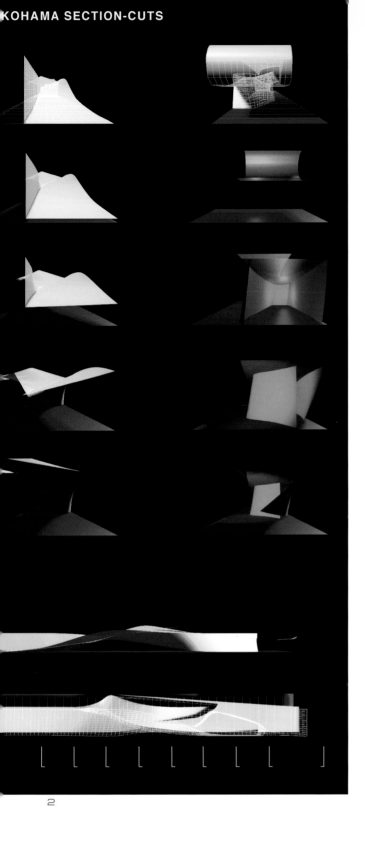

2

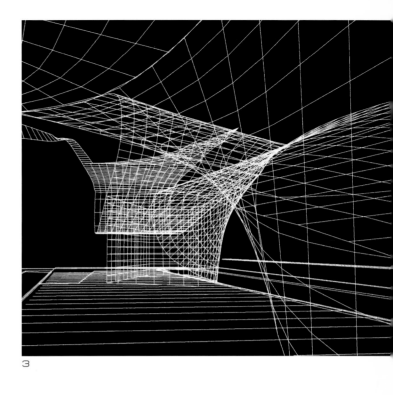

3

4

1 Program bands
2 Section diagrams
3 Wireframe view
4 View from terminal hall

VIEW FROM RESTAURANT

5

6

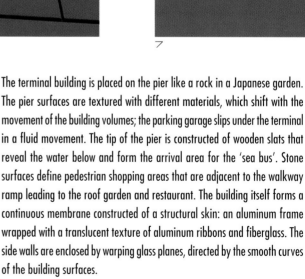

7

10-meter level, where they enter the visitors' decks and cafe. The surface of the cafe connects smoothly into the city restaurant located above, offering a spectacular view over the Yokohama Bay.

City Functions

The smooth transformation of the pier surface onto the twisting plane of the terminal allows the city's inhabitants to be inconspicuously drawn up the sloping plaza above the departure/arrival hall. Along this promenade they encounter the information center, exhibition hall, and shops. These shops have dual access—city pedestrians enter from the pier and travelers enter through the departure/arrival hall. Walking further, pedestrians pass the roof garden, the foyer of the salon of civic exchange, and proceed to a spacious restaurant overlooking the harbor.

The terminal building is placed on the pier like a rock in a Japanese garden. The pier surfaces are textured with different materials, which shift with the movement of the building volumes; the parking garage slips under the terminal in a fluid movement. The tip of the pier is constructed of wooden slats that reveal the water below and form the arrival area for the 'sea bus'. Stone surfaces define pedestrian shopping areas that are adjacent to the walkway ramp leading to the roof garden and restaurant. The building itself forms a continuous membrane constructed of a structural skin: an aluminum frame wrapped with a translucent texture of aluminum ribbons and fiberglass. The side walls are enclosed by warping glass planes, directed by the smooth curves of the building surfaces.

CYBER**SPACE**

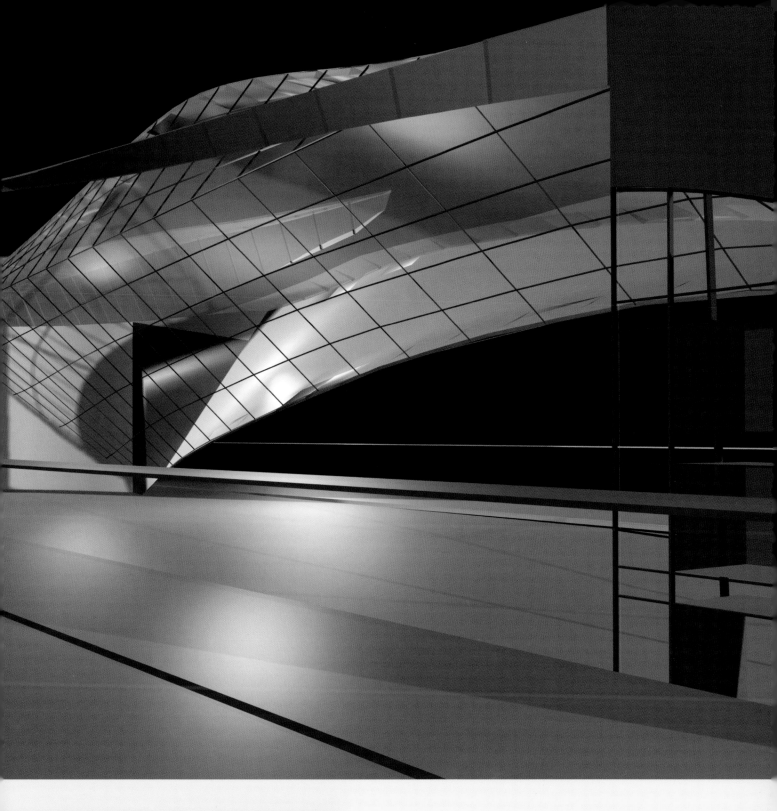

5 View from restaurant

6 View from inside terminal hall towards restaurant above

7 Perspective towards harbor and restaurant

8 Perspective towards shops

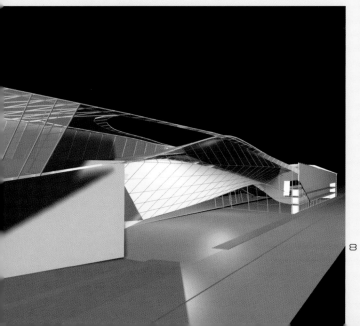

8

STUDIO 8 ARCHITECTS

EPHEMERAL URBAN FIELDS

Available from 'space-vending machines', field-packs generate a charged membrane that physically morphs and alters in transparency according to the frequency of an electric field. The introduction of an external charge, namely the electrical impulses fired during brain activity, alters the equilibrium, reconfiguring the field according to occupational requirements. The result is a telekinetic control system that creates an endless spatial dialogue of rhythmic light and movement with the environment.

An electric field can retain heat, repel water particles, and modulate temperature and light, in much the same ways that more physical barriers do. Its intangibility and variform coverage, however, liberate us from the archaism of immobile and unyielding architecture, suggesting new and virtual means of 'space-making', while questioning the social economics of personalized space and city planning laws.

All that is needed is an electric socket. As a result, space-making will become the ultimate 21st century throwaway consumer product.

1

1   Top view field reconfiguring
2   Diagrams of virtual morphing
3   Telekinetic control system
4   Looking through membrane
5   Cyber inhabitation

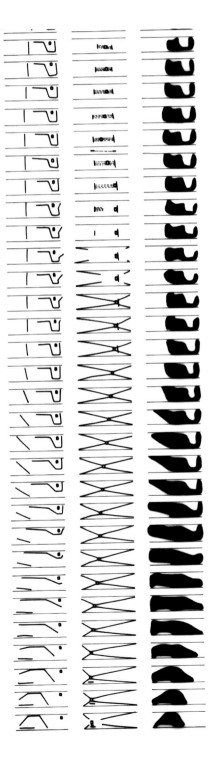

2

3

4

5

LAB + BATES SMART

FEDERATION SQUARE

Federation Square is a large-scale civic development, occupying more than a city block (3.5 hectares), and is currently under construction in the center of Melbourne, Australia. The project is a complex mix of cultural institutions, civic space, and commercial activities. Federation Square attempts the creation of a new urban order, capable of adapting to changing activities and social programs, whilst maintaining real links to an existing metropolitan context. This ambition is approached by strategies that produce coherence out of difference and materialize the invisible connections so essential to any dynamic urban center. In the true spirit of Federation, this design brings together distinct elements and activities, forming a complex ensemble based upon the unique and the collective.

1

1   Aerial render montaged onto city site
2   Internal perspective of south atrium
3   Composite plan

2

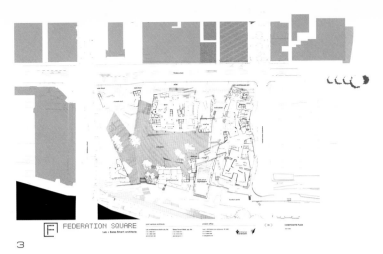

FEDERATION SQUARE
Lab + Bates Smart: architects

COMPOSITE PLAN

3

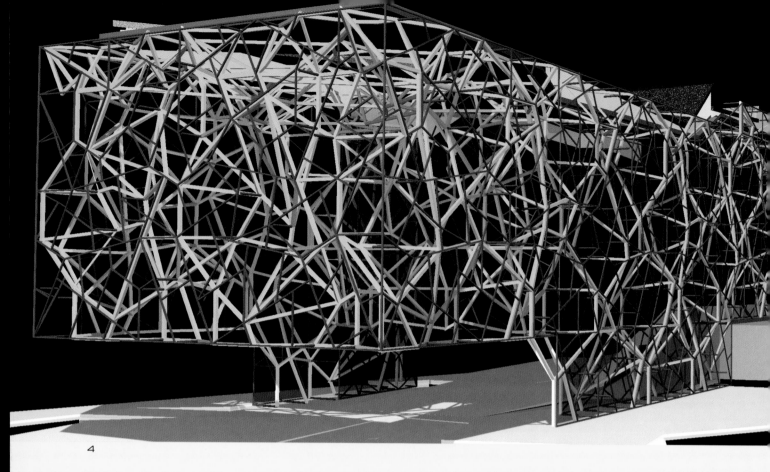

4

5

4 Study render of atrium

5 Internal render of National Gallery of
Victoria (NGV): Australian art foyer

6 Russell Street elevation

7 Flinders Street elevation

8 Facade wrap

YARRA RIVER

FLINDERS STREET

RUSSELL STREET ELEVATION

0 5 10   20   30

6

FLINDERS STREET ELEVATION

0 5 10   20   30

7

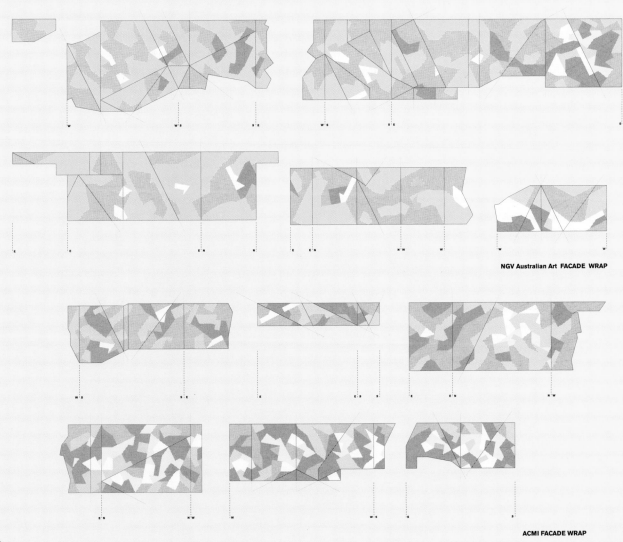

W   W S   S E   W S   S E   E

E   E   E N   N   E   E N   N W   W   W   W

NGV Australian Art FACADE WRAP

W S   S E   E   E S   S   E   E N   N W

E N   N W   W   W S   S

ACMI FACADE WRAP

8

OOSTERHUIS.NL

FLORIADE NH PAVILION

Instrumental Building

The multimedia pavilion (Noord-Holland pavilion) is a building body that can be played by its users. The users activate light, sound, images, and the behavior of the body. The building body becomes an instrument.

All electronic media are immersed in the interior skin, and if not activated, the body is in standby mode. When a visitor enters the body, a variety of sensors detect this and activate the local multisensory behavior. The visitor is aware of the response of the body. The full trajectory becomes a 30-minute conversation between visitor and building body. The content of the conversation is the various real-time characteristics of Noord-Holland in relation to the Floriade flower exhibition.

The building as an instrument offers much more than a passive consumption of a multimedia experience. Immediately after the visitor passes the lights, the sounds fade away again and images become blurred, and, if it is not triggered again, the body reverts to standby mode. The building body is constantly calculating and recalculating itself; there is never a completely static moment. There is slow movement and there is fast movement, but never a complete standstill.

After having followed the visitor's trajectory for some 20 meters, the building body gradually zips up to exclude outside air and daylight from the interior experiences. Now the electronic media takes over, and the visitor is drawn though a sequence of sectors of very different characteristics.

The visitors activate the behavior, the building body reacts to the flow of visitors. The trajectory is a journey from the real to the virtual and back to reality. The journey is specific to each visitor, thanks to the real-time programming. When the visitor leaves the building, the electronic media fade out, the body unzips.

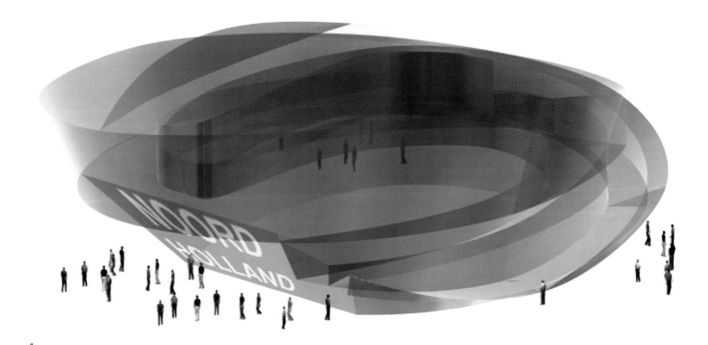

1

1 Building body is completely made of
 aluminum, welded together and forming
 one continuous skin
2 Side view of the aluminum unibody;
 exterior and interior skin are sandwiched
 together
3 The continuity of the 300-meter long
 trajectory, one continuous movement by
 connecting exit and entrance

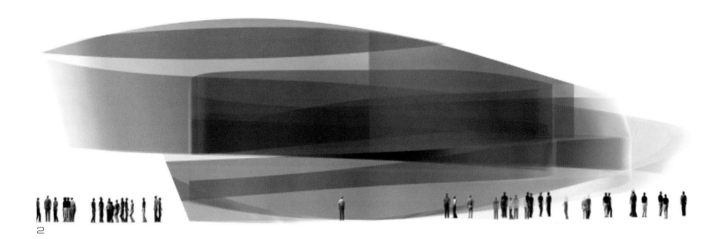

2

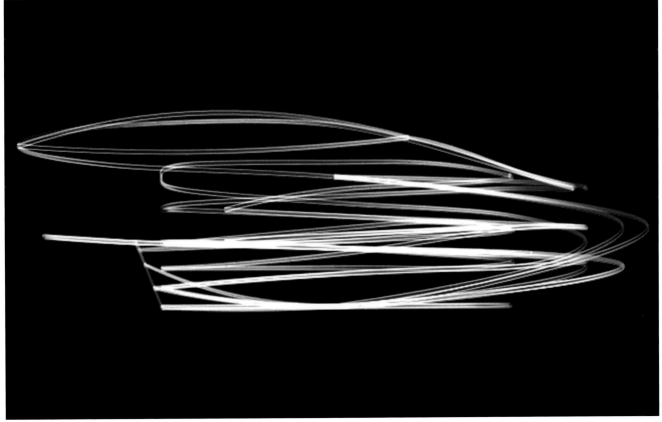

3

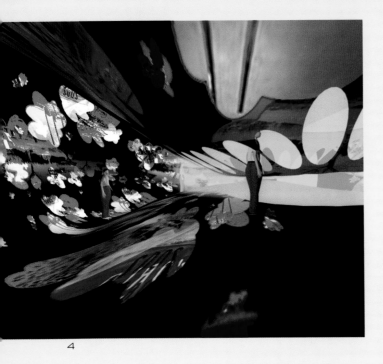

4 Central spot of the body is dive space; visitors experience a spectacular panoramic video and lightshow

5 The 300-meter long, three-dimensional folded whirling trajectory leads up towards dive space

6 Virtual landscapes project on reclining floor, sides, and ceiling; horizontal side cuttings reveal the real landscape

7 Blue is used for chromakey capturing of visitors; these video-grabbed pictures are inserted in virtual worlds

8 Wet point of view of water-rich Noord-Holland

4

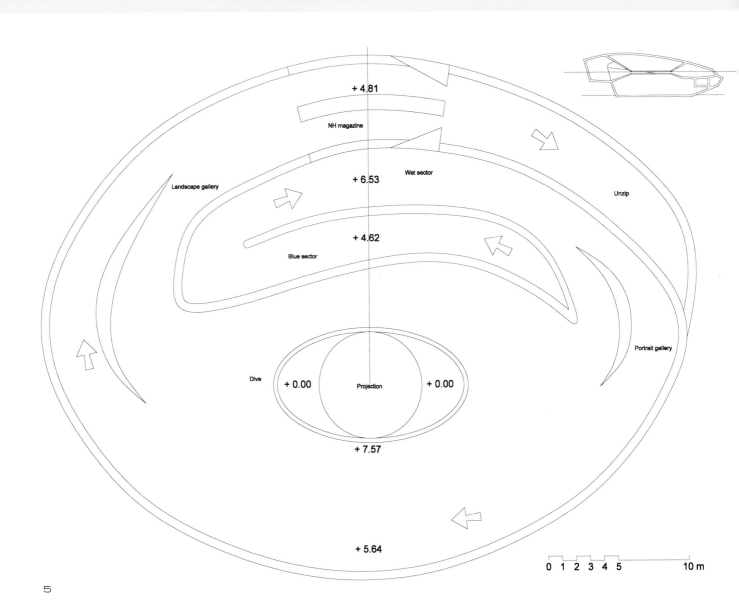

5

CYBER**SPACE**

6

7

8

LAB ARCHITECTURE STUDIO

FUTURE GENERATIONS UNIVERSITY

Future Generations University (FGU) was a proposal for a new university on the central coast of New South Wales, Australia, which was to be uniquely founded on principles of environmental sustainability, and whose scope encompassed the master planning of a new campus town for up to 6,000 inhabitants. The staging of the project whose development over time was based upon evolutionary intensification, not incremental zoning, thereby positively engaging all the potential forces of change: amendment, alteration, and adaptation during the process of development itself.

The images show the manner in which the various functional programs were initially established as fields of activity, forming an entire meshed matrix to maximize the interactions, and hence potential productive and unexpected relations, between constituent elements.

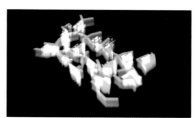

2

3

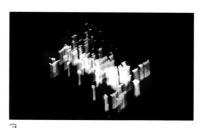

4

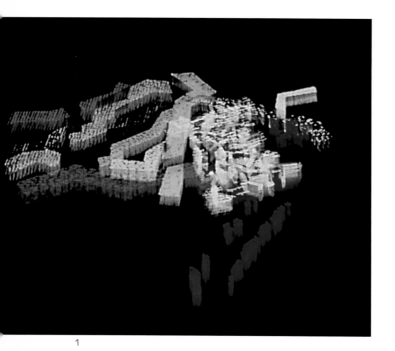

1

5

1 Botanic conservation gardens and composite building massing

2 Commercial matrix

3 Technologies and community matrix

4 Commercial matrix (time-based overlay)

5 Composite (master) plan for overall site including gardens, building programs, waste and ecology systems, vehicle and movement systems

6 Matrix elements—programmatic, operational, and phased implementation

A faculties

A1 intercultural communication

A2v manufactured ecologies

A3 sustainable management

A4 community

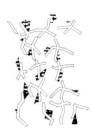

B technologies

C culinary activity/social activity

D common facilities

E administration/care activities

F circulation/shear lines

G residential accommodation

H zones of flux

I common facilities/temporary expansion

J commercial rental tenants

K retail service nodes

LAB ARCHITECTURE **STUDIO**

dECOi

GATESHEAD THEATRE

The sensual, flowing form of this project resulted from a series of form-finding experiments carried out for Foster & Partners for the overarching carapace of a tri-theatre complex. Challenged to devise new ways of deriving such forms elegantly, the firm did not so much 'design' the form as create methods by which the form could find itself—as a series of forces acting on elastic surfaces. The slight indeterminacy of the process was nonetheless highly precise, since it was developed in conjunction with mathematicians using extremely accurate three-dimensional engineering software. This marks a shift away from auto-determinism as a creative strategy.

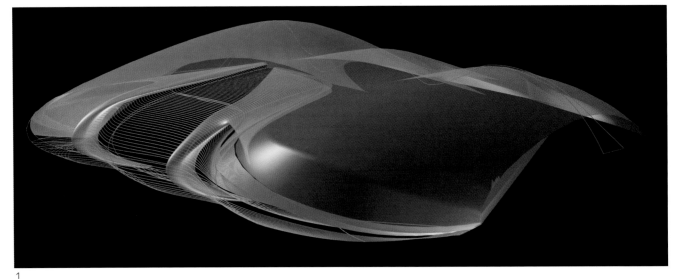

1

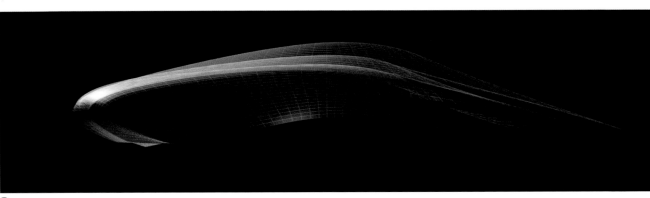

2

1&3 Perspective

2 Side elevation

4 Plan view

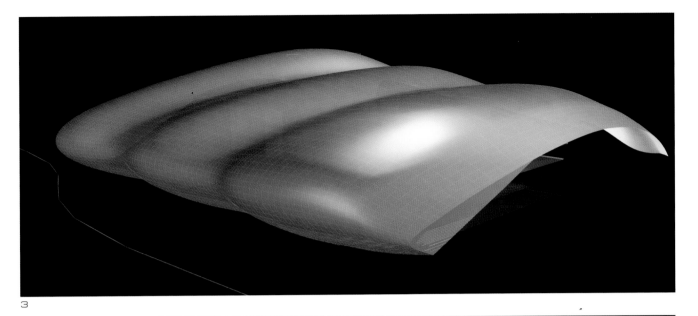

3

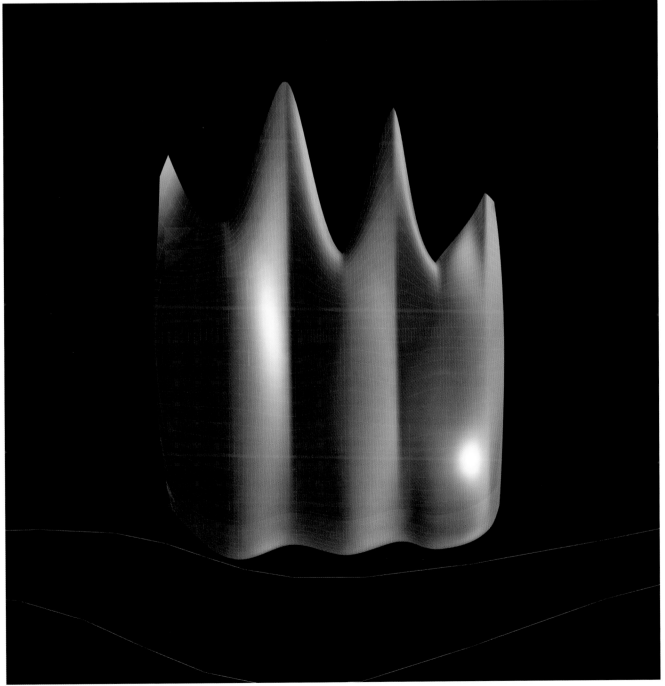

4

GOTEBORG: THE MUSEUM OF GLOBAL CULTURE 1998

In *The Question Concerning Technology*, Heidegger (1955) refers to the culture of man as a development that expresses itself both in art and science. Art is described here as the spiritual manifestation of this culture, science as the 'theory of the real'. Theory here can be thought of as observation (*Betrachtung*) and the notion of the real as 'of that which works', or of the verb 'to do', which goes back to the Greek term 'thesis'—the setting, place, position. The 'real' can be seen as an interacting network of surveyable related causes. Thus the new sciences could be described as a cultural expression that observes that which works, a network, a place, architecture.

Sitescape

The integration of the museum in the site, as well as the combination and confrontation of architecture, art, and science, forms an interesting challenge. The interest lies in the investigation of textures. Rather than Corbusier's *piloti* structure of 1930, which floated the building over the site, the firm proposes to develop a museum of interweaving programs, which are integrated within the landscape and become part of the urban geography.

This structure forms interweaving layers representing spatial, political, social, economic, and cultural influences. The layers form a dynamic system that connects and informs in an interweaving structure, represented in the matrix that replaces the Euclidean two-dimensional grid. Each layer has a programmatic imprint: the small square layer intersects with and connects to the large square exhibition layer. At the intersection point of the two layers, the museum transforms from a public space with library, meeting space, and workshops, into an interactive exhibition space, thus fluidly connecting as well as separating those two worlds.

The notion of time and space has been studied for many years in science. The introduction of time into our spatial experience of architecture will result in spaces consisting of a series of dynamic frames, of shifting horizons, which will transform the common notions of architectural elements like the wall, the door, the facade, and so on.

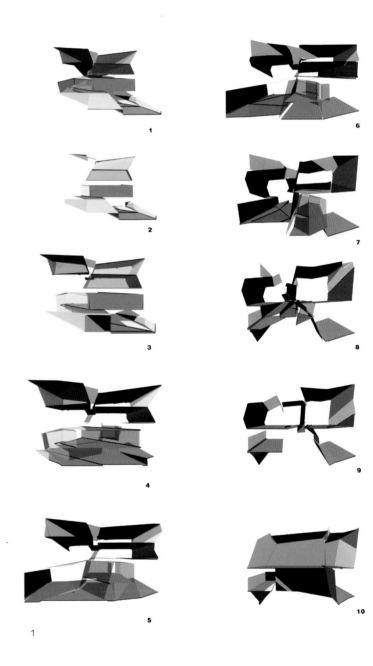

1

1 Three-dimensional section cuts through museum's twisting bands

2 Exploded axonometric

3 Exhibition hall

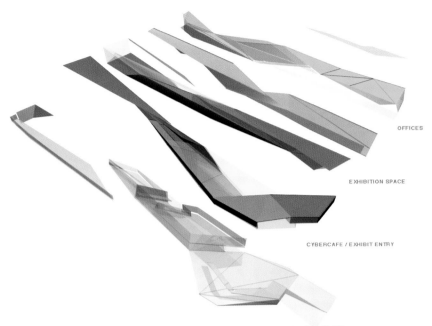

OFFICES

EXHIBITION SPACE

CYBERCAFE / EXHIBIT ENTRY

DIGITAL LIBRARY / WORKSHOPS

2

3

ARCHI-**TECTONICS**

4

5

CYBER**SPACE**

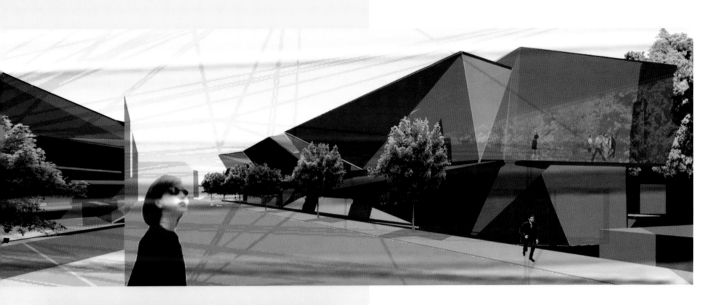

The introduction of light slots in the horizontal as well as the vertical planes will provide indirect light reflecting on the walls and floor, thus creating a spectacular play of daylight, constantly transforming the spatial experience of the museum. The introduction of recycled materials adds to the texture of the building, providing innovative maintenance-free solutions, while adding to the durability of the structure. In that spirit, the typology proposes the building as a landscape—a datascape integrated in the site.

Virtual textures relate to the constant flow of communication and new media. We can no longer visualize the 'real-time' space of communication that connects each of us to a global informational matrix. Our messages occupy the 'D-Zone', the belt around the Earth where satellites circle. The new computer network spaces, such as the World Wide Web, bring us more information on a broader level. These communication networks change the importance of the location or site of the built structure. Buildings can thus be located anywhere in this global matrix: in the desert, or underground in the metropolis. They are thus no longer concerned with a representation of power but rather form 'nodes' in the global network of information systems. The Museum of World Culture, with its electronic library, digital archive, and interactive exhibits, will become one of these global 'nodes' in the ongoing discussion of the relevance of art and architecture.

6

7

4 Museum inserted in site; entry facade with cyber cafe and digital library
5 Exhibition space with view to street
6&7 View from garden cafe to library

ARCHI-**TECTONICS**

SHUBIN + DONALDSON

GROUND ZERO I

The client, Ground Zero, founded in 1994, has quickly risen in the ranks of corporate branding, with advertising spots for ESPN2, Porsche, Virgin Group, and Activision.

The interior features a processionary, 9.5-foot-high ramp leading down from the elevated second floor entryway. As guests, clients, and staff make their way down the ramp, and through the entire length of the working 'hall', they are exposed to the ever-changing palette of the agency's work projected on a series of theatrical scrims spanning the width of the space. The 'soul of the creative machine' is revealed to all who enter the agency.

1   Photo of ramp
2   Conceptual digital model of ramp
3   Digital rendering down ramp
4-7 Digital conceptual visualization

1

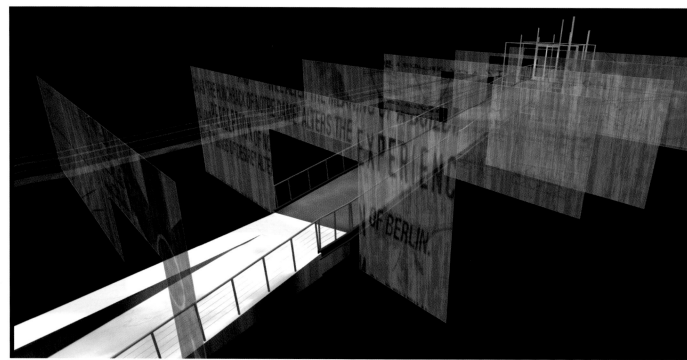

2

3

4

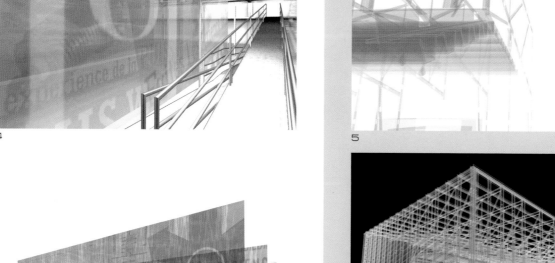

5

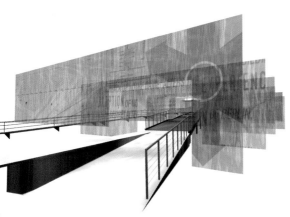

6

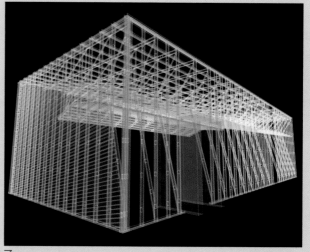

7

SHUBIN + DONALDSON

GROUND ZERO II

The original truss forms used in Ground Zero I were used to create a spine inside Ground Zero II. The trusses are joined by a series of metal-clad serpentine walls, which weave throughout the floor plan. These two entities intersect and combine to create new spaces.

These new and dramatic subspaces take form to produce fantastically shaped rooms, corridors, sculptures, and nooks. Among the most dramatic of these subspaces is the conference room, the walls of which ultimately extend beyond and carve out the existing warehouse wall to form an exterior entry that culminates on the sidewalk.

1

2

1 Digital rendering of exterior
2 Digital rendering of conference room
3-6 Digital conceptual visualization

3

4

5

6

SHUBIN + DONALDSON

ASYMPTOTE ARCHITECTURE

GUGGENHEIM VIRTUAL MUSEUM

The Solomon R. Guggenheim Museum commissioned Hani Rashid and Lise Anne Couture of Asymptote Architecture to design and implement a new venue in cyberspace. The first phase of the Guggenheim Virtual Museum (GVM) is being launched as part of a three-year initiative. The GVM will not only house and connect all of the Guggenheim museums worldwide but will also be the first museum to contain art generated exclusively within and for the Internet.

The museum will contain ongoing special exhibits and a digital architecture archive, as well as three-dimensional spaces linking the various 'first reality' museums and amenities. The project will consist of navigable three-dimensional spatial entities accessible on the Internet as well as a real-time interactive component installed at the Soho Guggenheim located in New York City.

For Asymptote this important new work brings forward their interests in merging technological possibilities with human experience and spatial manufacture.

When speaking of architecture today, Asymptote believes there are two conditions to consider: first, the physical space of architecture as it has been traditionally defined, in terms of enclosure, form, and permanence; and secondly, another architecture now surfacing within digital domains, that of the virtual.

According to Asymptote, buildings, institutions, objects, and space are now being constructed, navigated, experienced, comprehended, and altered in their virtual states, effectively forming an extension to physical space. This is a new architecture of liquidity, flux, and mutability, predicated on technological advances and fueled by the basic human need to probe the unknown. Asymptote asserts that the path that both these architectures, the real and

1 Interface study for navigational system for gallery components
2 Navigational interface study for virtual venues where various physical locals can be accessed
3 Morphing study for Plaza component

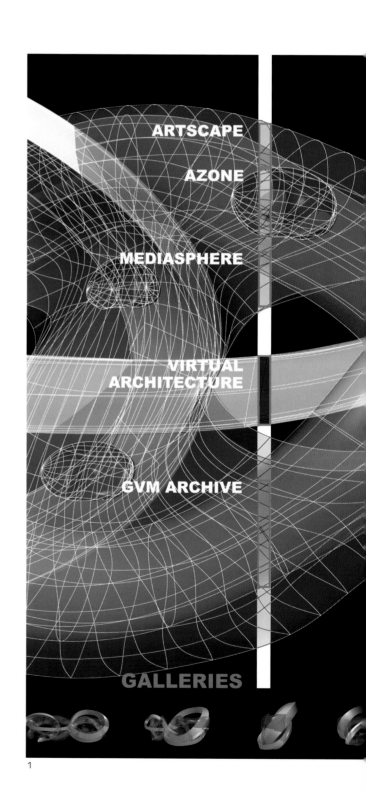

1

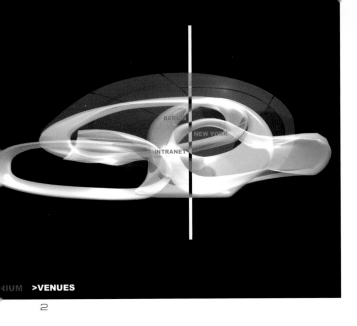

RIUM >VENUES

2

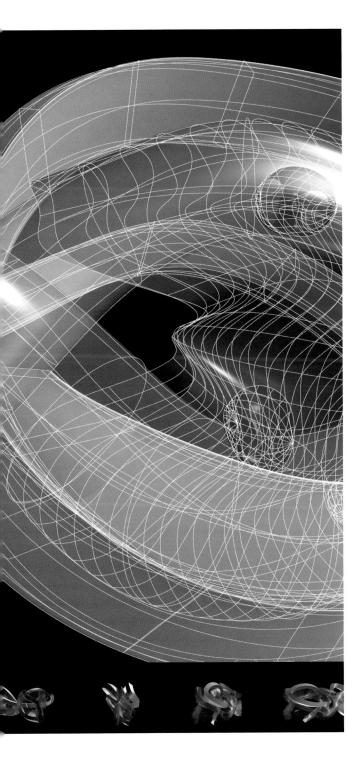

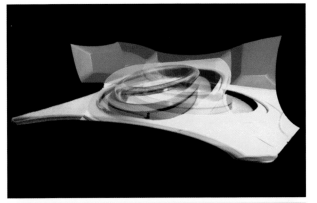

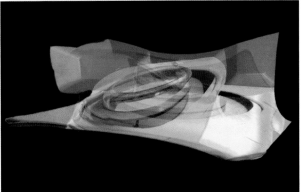

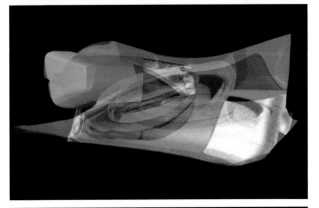

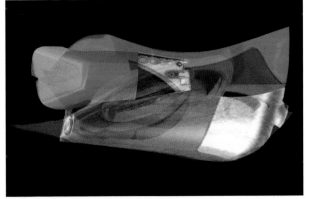

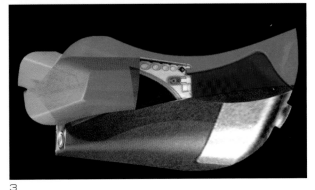

3

ASYMPTOTE **ARCHITECTURE**

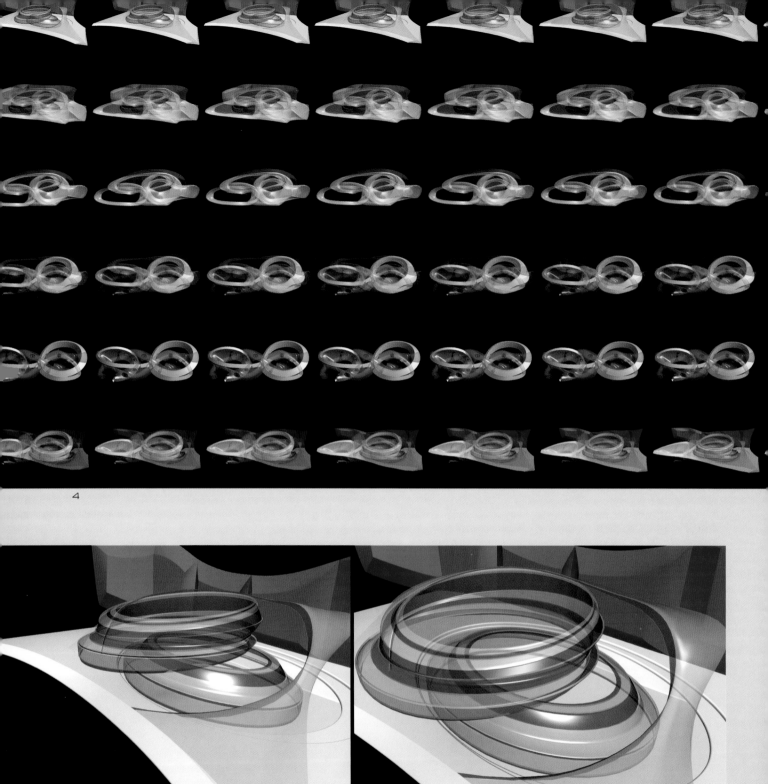

4

5

the virtual, will inevitably take will be one of convergence. They say that historically architecture has struggled with this dialectic of the real and the virtual; architecture's stability and actuality are always being tempered by their metaphysical and poetic condition.

Today's computers, global networks, and digital tools are the critical means by which we navigate this trajectory into the future. The Guggenheim Virtual Museum, as envisioned by Asymptote, originates and surfaces from such a possibility, where the museum's historic architectural vanguard and its valued pedagogical and cultural dimension serve to form a unique scaffolding for the museum of the future.

The Guggenheim Virtual Museum, utilizing state-of-the-art technologies, will emerge as a new architectural work, fusing information, space, art, commerce, and architecture as an event-driven internet experience. The resulting virtual architectural project will unite all the Guggenheim museums into a single, globally accessible architectural object, effectively positioned to be the first virtual architecture to emerge in the early 21st century.

CYBER**SPACE**

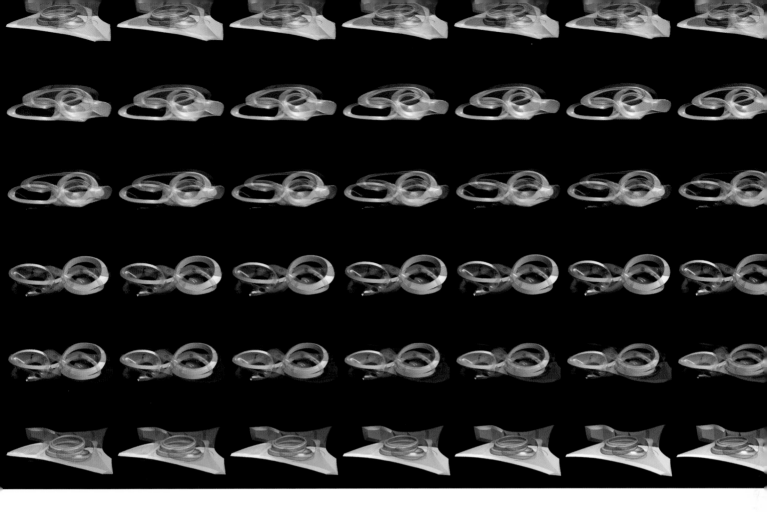

4 Morphing anatomy diagram for the three components of GVM

5 Plaza 'ring' study for virtual fly through to entry area

6 Architectural study of gallery component from two views

6

A ZONE [2B] / VIDEO ART / 1990–2000

7

8

9

10

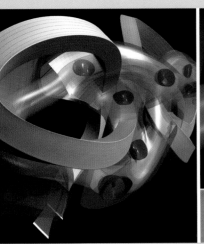

11

7 Portal entry to video art collection

8 Gallery architecture study

9 Exterior view of entry rings and virtual
   surveillance ticker

10 Interior view of atrium space and entry
   rings

11 Architectural designs for gallery
   environment

OOSTERHUIS.NL

HELSINKI MUSIC CENTER

Built on Bedrock Topography

The concept for the new Helsinki Music Center is clear and simple, and as a result features many interesting complications in the development of the building. The center is built on bedrock; the loose landfill was taken away and the whole site was cleared. This bedrock has a most intriguing topology; a hidden landscape that relates strongly to the city structure of Helsinki.

The formerly hidden topography was then undressed and the program of the Helsinki Music Center was constructed right on top of the bedrock, which remains uncovered and bare in the canyon. Building right on the bedrock implies that the ground floor is like a landscape. It is never exactly horizontal—there is always a slight slope, but never more than the programmatic content allows. It also allows physically challenged people to move about in their wheelchairs.

1 Roof park covered with varied tundra vegetation in summer; music played inside lightens up concert hall
2 Wireframe model of existing topology of bedrock
3 Concert hall alien landing on and merging with glacier skin

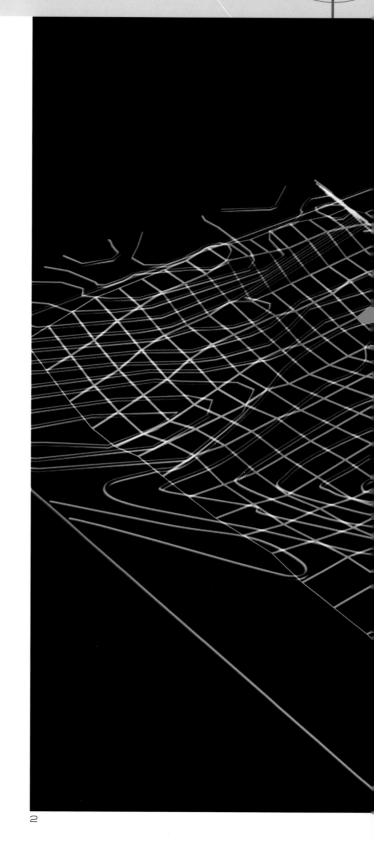

1

2

3

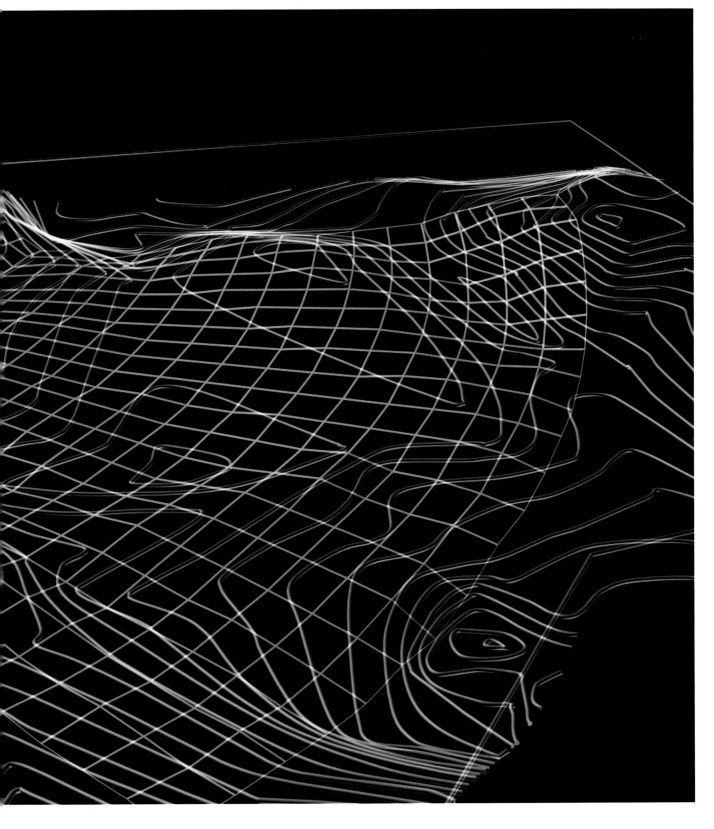

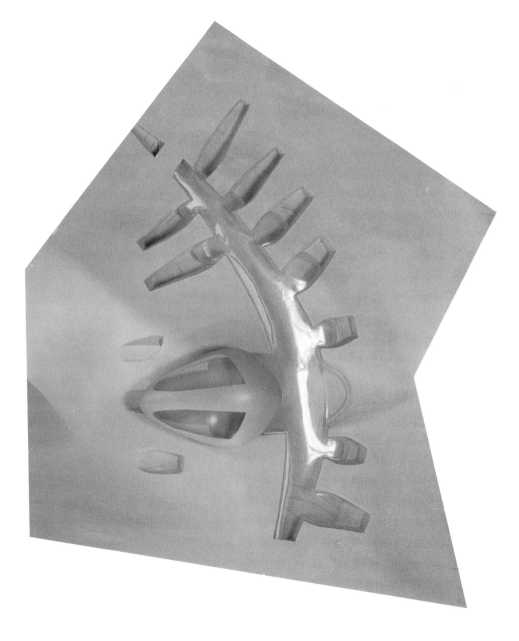

4

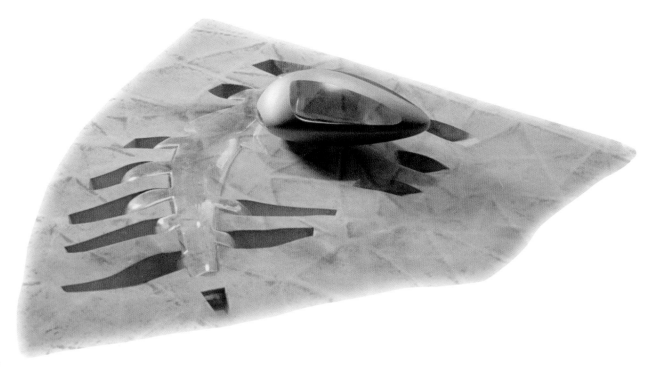

5

4 Fusion of concert hall alien with shiny
transparent glacier

5 Fresh snow covering the park in winter;
public winter garden in the glacier used as
passage

6 Bedrock topography, park, canyon, glass
glacier, and concert hall

6

In response to current technological and cultural landscapes, consider an architecture of flows: flows of energy, materials, occupancy, and information—an interactive, filtered space with an open-ended arterial network of services, a dematerialized architecture, a filter or membrane intervening and responding with only enough presence to allow the occupants environmental control. Buckminster Fuller has termed such a process of technological evolution 'ephemeralization', where doing more for less can lead to an implosion of functions, one into another, until only a single, fine, multi-functional envelope or 'skin' takes the place of the separate cultures of structure, aesthetics, and service systems.

The HyperHouse is a campsite for new nomads, a hyperflexible space designed to facilitate connection and change, where information is precious, occupation and lifestyle shift constantly, and the little time one has left for friends and family must be spent well. Voice and gesture control domestic functions from the vacuum cleaner to the patterning and ventilation of the glass building skin.

The infiltration of electronics into the vocabulary of building brings with it the capacity for connection, not only of all systems within the building, but also of the building itself to the surrounding world. As well as being a climatic filter, the bounding membrane can also act as a communications filter or interface, transmitting television images, animated patterns, and messages. The HyperHouse functions as a dynamic interface. The connection may simply be enhanced communication with other people outside the building, or it can be interaction with, or a response to, the emission of data from any source or algorithm; building as a dynamic topological process, a seismic register.

As a media skin for the occupants, the identity and character of the house evolves as it responds to, and stores data from, the needs and use patterns of the occupants. Favorite ventilation patterns, privacy and illumination settings, and graphic envelope displays forge for the house the comfortable character of a well-worn glove. It is a space crafted by information. The facade can be a media strip, a flow of projections, no longer a static event, but a momentary and constantly moving one.

A single integrated loom cables services to all domestic spaces. It uses dry-break, self-sealing, spillproof couplers, like the liquid petroleum gas (LPG) hose at your local petrol or gas station, to allow the rapid connection of any service.

The kitchen is a mobile appliance, able to be located at any point along the service loom from the central living area to the deck or any other part of the house. It is made up of compact interchangeable and upgradeable modules for food preparation.

1   Exterior view
2&3   Skin
4   Skin and kitchen

1

2

3

4

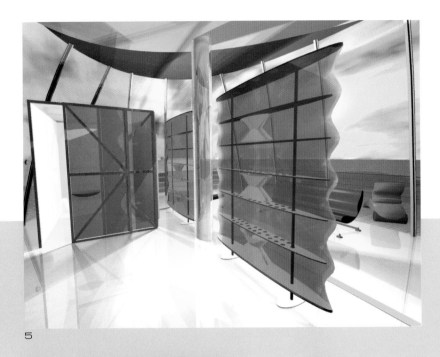

5

6

7

5 Electronic interior screens
6 TV skin
7 MVR Bathroom Module
8 Bedroom

8

TRISTAN D'ESTREE STERK & ROBERT WOODBURY

IDEA CLOUD

We have to build up a counter power to the monotony of 'industrial work'. This can't be done without architecture. We have to ... save the human being who does, from morning to night, only a monotonous type of work. If I should say my final words, I should say that, one of the great problems for an architect today is to save the human being; to make individualism of collectivism.

Alvar Alto, architect—an interview from *The Oral History Of Modern Architecture*

Architecture is no game. It is an activity that has imposed upon it the great responsibilities of serving and sheltering, both physically and mentally, the people who inhabit its spaces. Alvar Alto's words serve to identify these responsibilities and they frame architecture, not just as an industrial pursuit, but also as a 'human' pursuit where the monotonous can be shed and where an individual can reach into a domain of whimsical delight. Architecture needs to be individualistic. It needs to be free, fresh, and light, and to go further it needs to surpass any of the limits that systematic technologies impose—be they physical or digital.

The human within: if there is any strength in this project, it lies in the way that it addresses the different types of space that humans (individuals and collectives) occupy. It recognizes that people have the opportunity to inhabit more than one type of space at any one point in time, and it actively produces a space that lets the 'human within' affect the architecture of an entire building.

Our feelings and thoughts affect the ways we interact with environments. For example, the way we walk or march through a space has the potential to influence the mood of a space, purely through physical action. In this light, the mass of a body, its movement, actions, and sounds, can all be used to affect the way spaces are 'virtually' configured. This is especially relevant to spaces that attempt to straddle both the physical and virtual worlds; it is in these sorts of spaces that designers have the clear opportunity to use totally ephemeral yet meaningful feelings to generate a realizable cybernetic architecture. The Idea Cloud is such a space. In effect, it brings the architecture of our mind into the physical spaces we occupy. We cannot help but act the way we think, and by detecting these actions, sensor technologies, combined with digital networks and hundreds of programmable hydraulic units, enable the Idea Cloud to react to variations in the environment.

Alto's words come with serious intent. If anything, as architects we need to recognize that our architecture, whether physical, virtual, or cybernetic (a mix of the former two), needs to address and acknowledge the humans within.

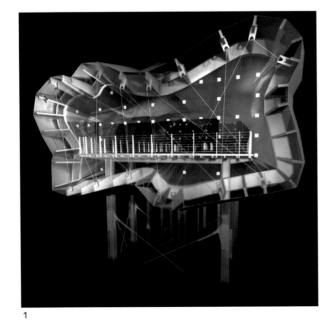

1

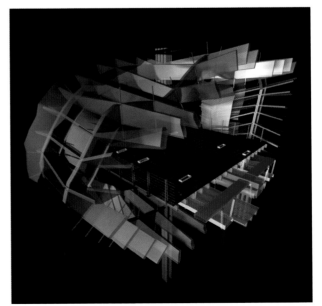

2

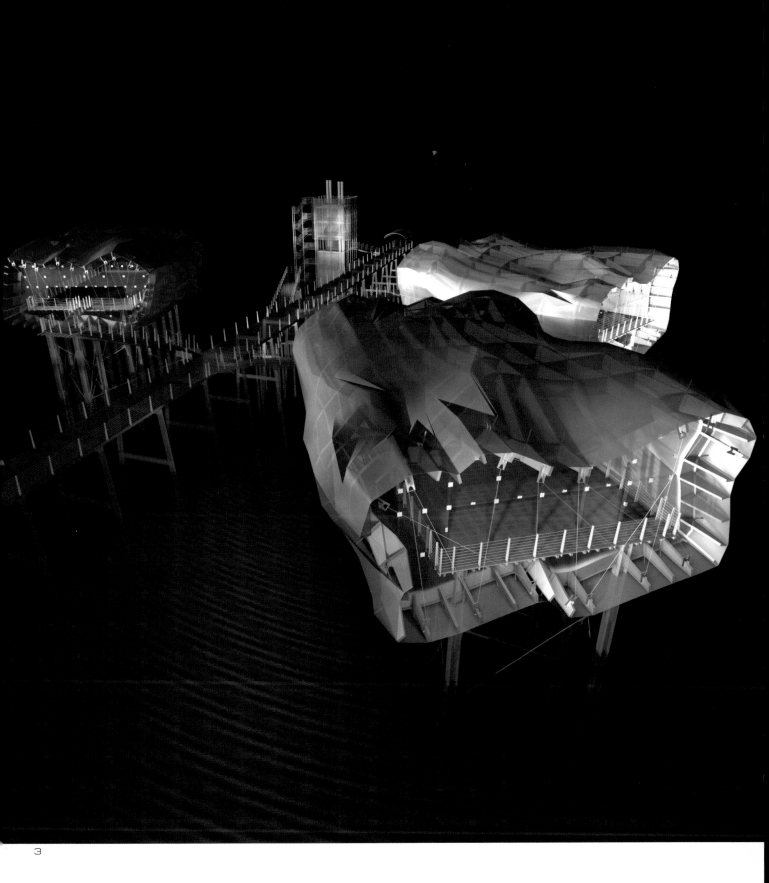

3

1-3 Idea Cloud

TRISTAN D'ESTREE STERK **& ROBERT WOODBURY**

4

5

6

4-6   Idea Cloud

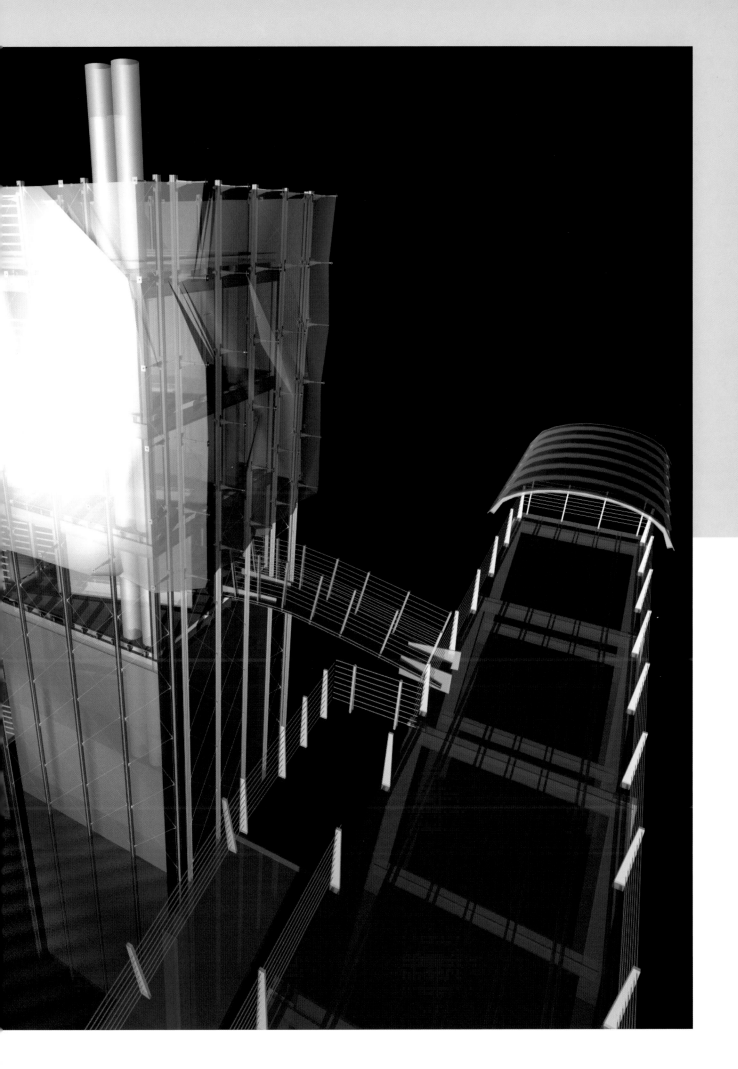

TRISTAN D'ESTREE STERK **& ROBERT WOODBURY**

STEPHEN PERRELLA, HYPERSURFACE SYSTEMS

INSTITUTE FOR ELECTRONIC CLOTHING

The Institute for Electronic Clothing project was developed by Stephen Perrella and Tony Wong in 1990. The proposed program's siting is undetermined and aspires to indeterminacy. The nonlinear process used to develop the architecture problematises authorship by implementing an invented strategy called 'whether conditions'. Meaning here is contingent—non-metaphysical—and operates as an 'other'. The project's meaning does not derive from normative metaphysical relations *vis-a-vis* 'strong' referents, metaphors, or narrative structures. Design decisions are weakly determined by resonance and effects occurring within specific meaning frames, within and beyond the sphere of the project. Intention does not control the development of the form.

Grafting is a technique employed in the 'whether conditions' process to deconstruct existing texts. Grafted diagrams used in the initial and later phases interrogate strong referential meaning. In this practice, all aspects of the project are in a 'graphemmatic' condition: the condition of two- and three-dimensional imagery rendered undecidable.

In the Institute for Electronic Clothing, the program is the 'other' of the repressive programs of a contemporary, market-driven information culture. In the implementation of the 'whether conditions' process, diagrams derived from sources such as the travelling salesman problem in nonlinear optimization are graphemmatic devices whose original variables are reconfigured as they contribute to the development of an architectural program involving electronic clothing.

1

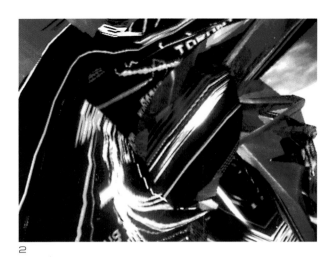

2

1-3   Institute for Electronic Clothing
      computer images

3

STEPHEN PERRELLA, **HYPERSURFACE SYSTEMS**

4

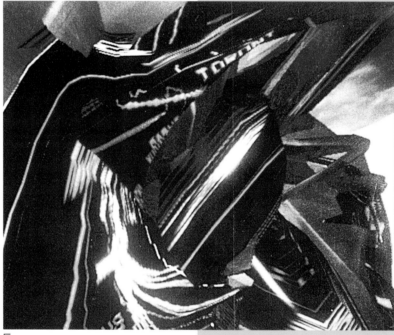

5

4-8 Institute for Electronic Clothing
computer images

6

7

8

STEPHEN PERRELLA, **HYPERSURFACE SYSTEMS**

STEPHEN PERRELLA, HYPERSURFACE SYSTEMS

THE MOEBIUS HOUSE STUDY

The Moebius House Study (by Stephen Perrella and Rebecca Carpenter) is an investigation into contemporary domesticity to reconsider dwelling for the new millennium. A preliminary investigation revealed that the pervasive use of technology in the home represents an ontological dilemma. Current house formats are no longer tenable because space and time are reconfigured by a lived informational geometry. Viewed solely in terms of Euclidean space, dwelling has become problematic as a result of media infiltrations—a force that implodes distance and then perplicates subjectivity as it enfolds viewer perception in an endless barrage of electronic images. This occurs in combination with, and yet is dissimilar to, the dynamics of teletechnology and computer-to-Internet connectivity. As home viewing narrows onto the television surface, it fuses with an image blitz to produce a perpetual present. Teletechnology contributes to a burrowing effect, altering the home as an exclusively interior condition. This battlefield of intersubjectivity renders problematic the notion of the dweller–consumer as an ego-construct-identity, which has traditionally been based upon an interiority divided from an exteriority and guided by an ideality.

The Moebius House Study for post-Cartesian dwelling is thus neither an interior space nor an exterior form. It is a transversal membrane that reconfigures binary notions of interior/exterior into a continuous, interwrapping median— a hypersurface facilitating proprioceptive experience, a radical empiricism more commensurate with the complexities of new-millennium modes of inhabitation.

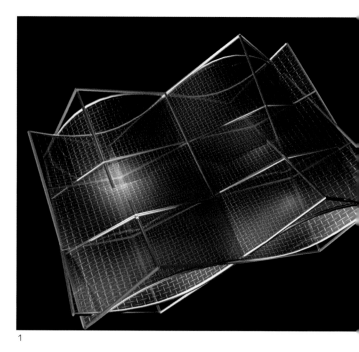

1

2

1&2 Hypersurface panel studies
3-6 Moebius House Study

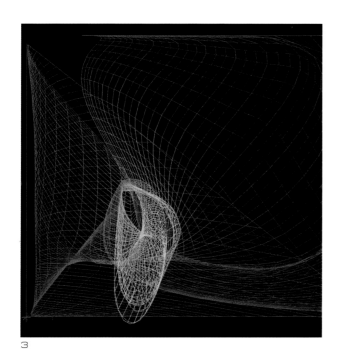

3

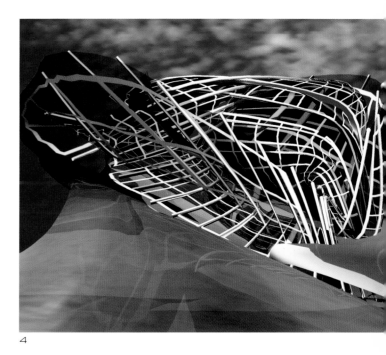

4

5

6

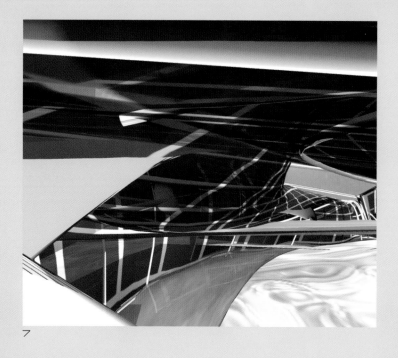

7

7, 8, 10 & 11   Moebius House Study

9   Hypersurface panel studies

9

8

10

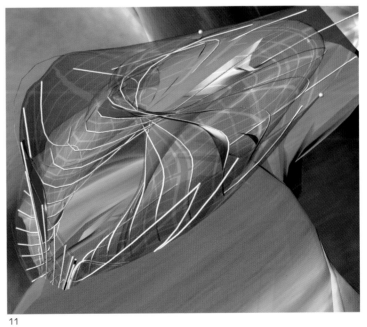

11

STEPHEN PERRELLA, **HYPERSURFACE SYSTEMS**

MUNICH AIRPORT, TERMINAL 2, COMPETITION ENTRY

Modern air travel can be a confusing and extremely stressful experience. Kohn Pedersen Fox's (London) competition entry for Munich Airport Terminal 2 has been designed to ease this task. The scheme aims to centralize the activities of the airport hub while creating a major civic space.

The airport has perhaps become the structure that affects the greatest numbers of people. It acts as a gateway into the local community for the arriving global community, and has effectively replaced the church and square, albeit on a megascale, as a gathering place for people from all walks of life. The expression of the airport can be seen as a celebration of mankind.

Kohn Pedersen Fox's design responds to the differing natures of distinct passenger types, and ensures that movement through the terminal is unimpeded, enabling travelers to find their way intuitively. The form of Terminal 2 takes the airfoil as its inspiration, and the long, wing-like roof signals the building's role as a new gateway to Munich.

The roof form of the new terminal reflects its three principal functions: check-in, market, and departure. A high, simple, lightweight, shell-like structure covers the check-in area, taking its form from the section of a cone. Gently bowed, its shallow curvature has been designed to utilize the segmented steel and aluminum building components. The inclined green roof is punched through with glass skylights that help to illuminate the shopping center beneath, and creates an interesting yet modest juxtaposition with the superstructure of the existing terminal. The building's internal elliptical form contains outwardly the check-in facilities, and inwardly retail facilities, creating a clear and logical entry hall that both expresses the excitement and grandeur befitting an airport, and provides a relaxing environment for the shopping center. In this way two clearly different spaces are created from one architectural form.

Extensive landscaping links Terminals 1 and 2 along the master plan axes, integrating the new building into the existing master plan, and culminating in garden spaces in the departure pier. Underground parking garages are provided close by, disguised by green roofs which add to the garden landscape of the artificial ground plane and minimize the impact on the surrounding landscape.

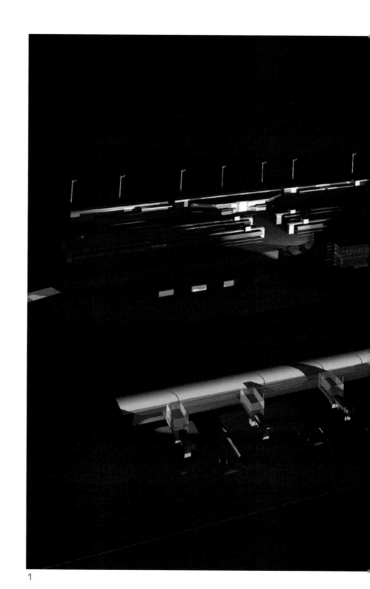

1

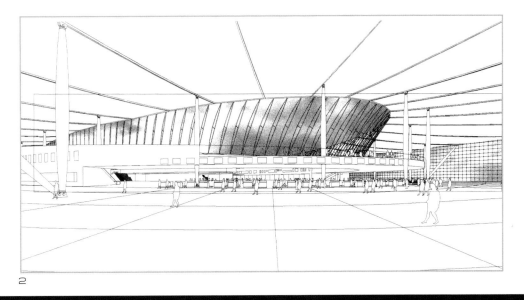

2

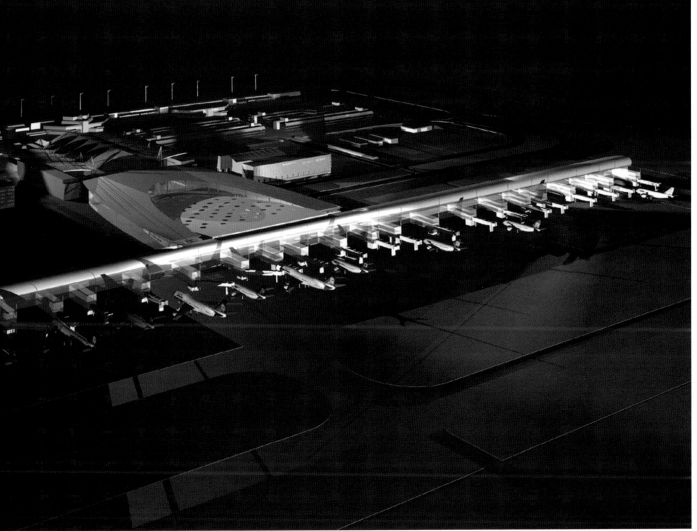

1   Aerial night view of airport terminal—
     computer rendering

2   Terminal interior looking towards check-in
     facilities—one point perspective computer
     sketch

KOHN PEDERSEN FOX **ASSOCIATES**

The design employs economical and durable finishes, and makes use of series system products, allowing expansion and flexibility without interruption to or major additional expense.

The Terminal 2 project set out to remove the labyrinthine aspect that dominates contemporary airports and air travel, and to create an architectural celebration of the joy of flight.

3

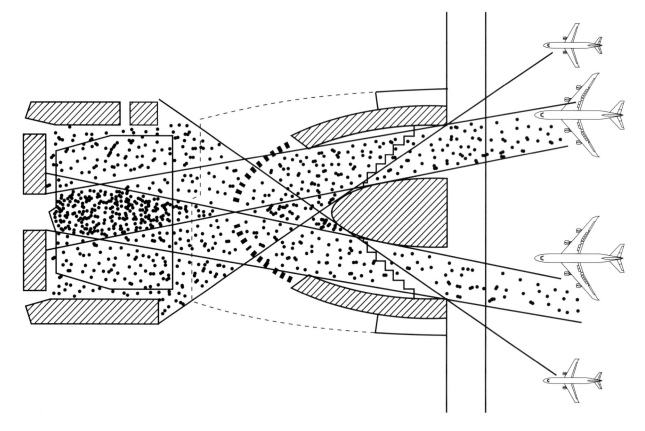

4

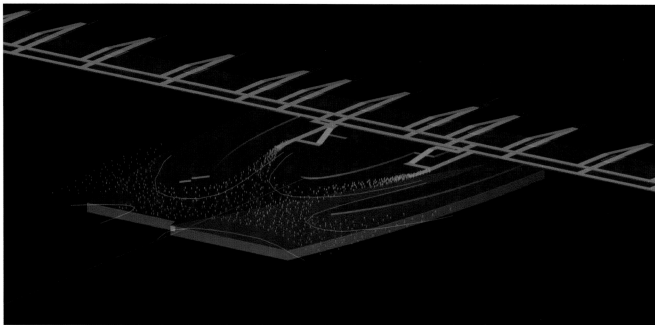

5

3 Terminal and boarding gate—axonometric
   computer sketch
4 Departure flow plan
5 Arrival flow diagram

6 Road level passenger drop-off—computer
   rendering
7 Departure concourse view—computer
   rendering

6

7

UN STUDIO
VAN BERKEL & BOS

MUSIC THEATER, GRAZ 1998-2003

Contemporary music and notational techniques interactively produce new forms of composition. Similarly, the interaction of architectural themes and structural organizations produces innovation in buildings and ideas. The design for the music faculty of the University of Graz (MUMUT) takes the spiral as its organizational principle. The spiral is intrinsically linked to the distribution of the program and to the theme of the music theater and its surroundings. The spiral dictates circulation, volume, and substance, and integrates the construction.

From Blob to Box and Back Again

The music faculty houses public functions relating to the performance of music, and private functions relating to teaching, training, and administration. These are both connected and separated in the spiral organization. The archetypal figure of the spiral has characteristics that are allied to music, such as rhythm, continuity, channeling, and directionality. The spiral organization allows for transitional zones that provide acoustic buffering. These zones also establish a secondary circulation system for performers, which is separate from the main, public route and which connects the private functions relating to the educational facilities.

The public program of the MUMUT is largely directed towards the park. The main entrance is situated on an inner court, around which various other faculties are grouped. This entrance is announced by a deep loop and raised terrace; its sloping surface provides a connection with the park. From the street, the park can be seen on the other side of the building. The underpass to the park is well lit through the void above it, made possible by the circulation system.

1

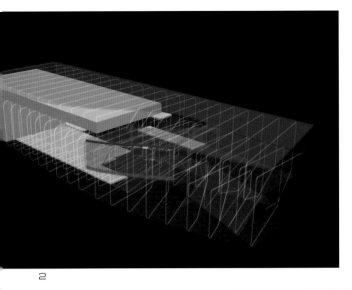

2

1 Foyer

2 Overlapping functions

3 Garden facade

3

UN STUDIO **VAN BERKEL & BOS**

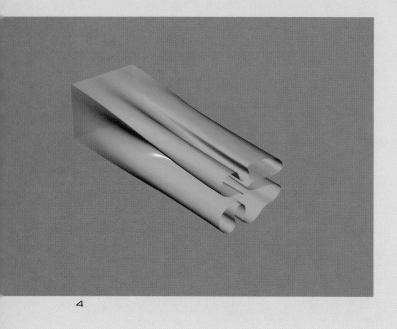

4

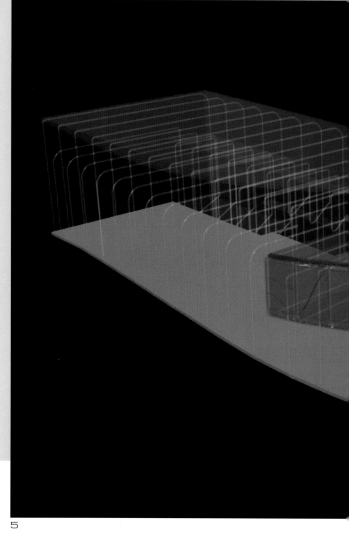

5

Centrally placed in the building is a buffered 'black box'—this is the auditorium, which can be flexibly used as workspace, concert hall, and music theater. The auditorium is reached from the main entrance on the ground floor via a foyer zone that slopes up to the first floor. Attached are a cafeteria, technical spaces, and dressing rooms. The auditorium, which floats above the park, has service spaces for the theater beneath it.

The spiral works as the organizing element of the MUMUT in much the same way that serialism does in contemporary music; the continuous line absorbs and regulates intervals and interruptions, changes of direction, and leaps of scale without losing its continuity. Objects hang on this line like laundry: glass, concrete, and installations.

The spiral transforms itself from blob to box and vice versa in an endless composition—it is simple, orthogonal, and horizontally oriented on one side and turns into a complex, smaller-scaled principle on the opposite side. Like an octopus, the spiral divides itself into a number of interconnected smaller spirals that take on a vertical and diagonal direction. Because of this organizing principle, which is also constructive, a fluent, column-free internal spatial arrangement is actualized, efficiently connecting spaces to each other.

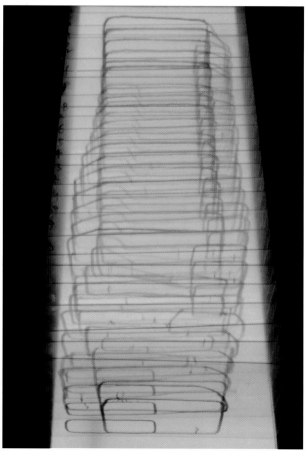

6

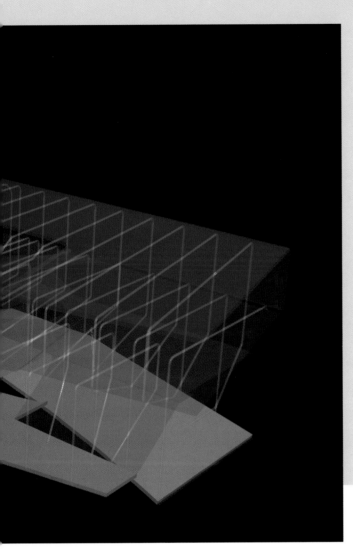

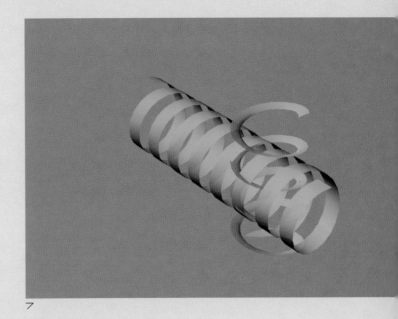

7

4 Octopus; from box to blob
5 Public area
6 Section model of spiral principle
7 Spiral concept
8 Public circulation

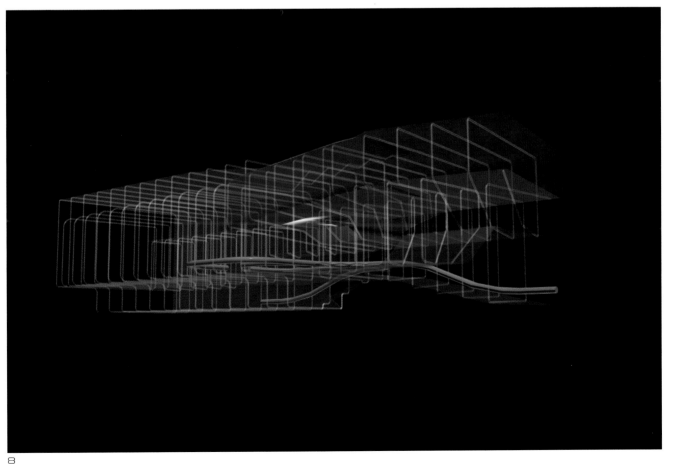

8

CESAR PELLI & ASSOCIATES

NATIONAL MUSEUM OF CONTEMPORARY ART 1996–2002

The National Museum of Contemporary Art is located on an irregular and extremely tight below-grade site on the island of Nakano, Japan, in a major cultural and artistic district. Cesar Pelli & Associates was requested to give the museum a prominent and distinctive image, not only for itself but to announce the entire cultural center. Conceived as a sculptural form, the lightweight stainless steel entrance acts as a counterpoint to the massive form of the neighboring Science Museum. The museum is distributed on three levels, the first being a public-free zone that is followed by two levels of gallery space.

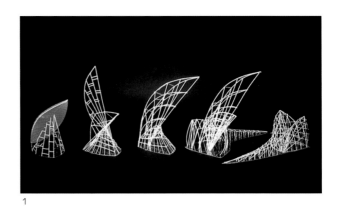

1

1 Study models of museum entrance
2 North view
3 East elevation
4 West view

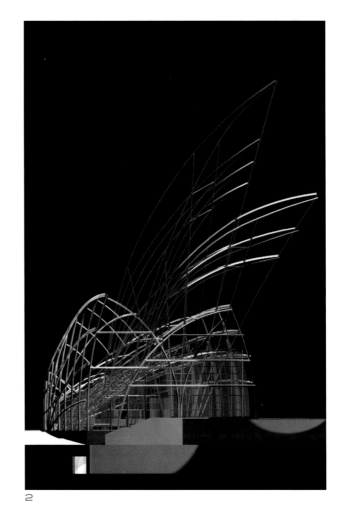

2

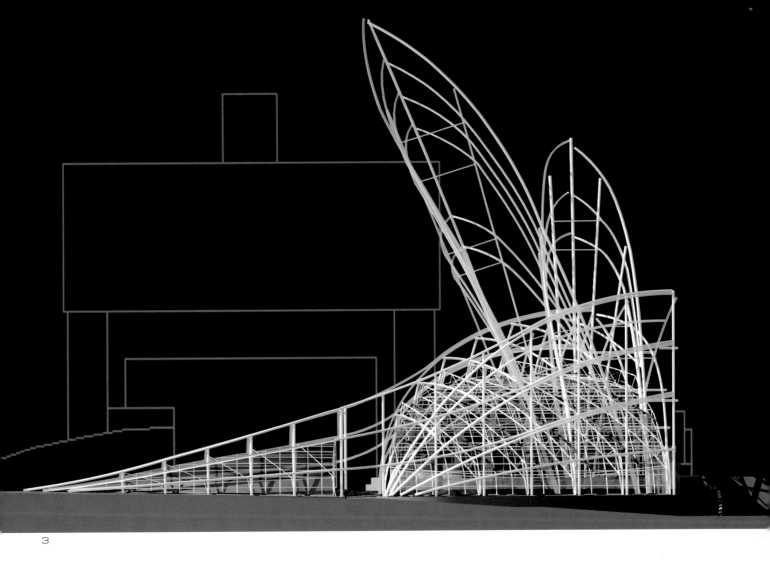

3

4

5

6

CYBER**SPACE**

5　View up to skylight

6　View of main public lobby

KOLATAN/ MAC DONALD STUDIO

OBSERVATORIUM FOR A POLDER

When Kolatan/Mac Donald were invited to contribute to the Observatorium's Polder Project in New York City, they saw it as an opportunity to extend their research into 'chimerical architectures' by testing a previous speculation at its largest architectural scale to date. This project was initially derived by transforming everyday objects such as a child's car seat, a phone receiver, and a computer mouse via recombinative logics that depend on the registration of similar and gradient attributes.

The project is located in an archipelago of small sand beach islands which register the tide differential providing a continually changing path to the Observatorium. The Observatorium is a double composite shell structure made of molded fiberglass layered in sections, giving the two shells varying degrees of transparency, translucency, and opacity. The shells operate simultaneously as enclosure, structure, and fenestration.

One enters through the 'dive-in'. As the water rises and falls, a water seal is created at the entry, requiring one to dive through the water during high tides, or wait until the water subsides in order to enter or exit dry. The cavity between the shells fills with rainwater from above, which mixes with the seawater from below. The water level is continuously modulated by the level of rainfall and the pressure differential between the two water sources. In certain instances this allows a person to be completely surrounded by water, as though in a bubble. The variation in water level also affects the transparency of the shells, and therefore the degree of privacy in the Observatorium. Parts of the inner and outer surfaces are coated with a soft gel; this material makes possible lounging activities such as sunbathing in the saddle of the roof, or sleeping in the interior space.

The program for the Observatorium is simply to provide escape in solitude from a city that has no beach and precious little horizontal surface.

jacuzzi/gel

bed/gel

A

A

B

B

entrance

1

1 Plan
2 Section A-A
3 Section B-B

KOLATAN/MAC DONALD **STUDIO**

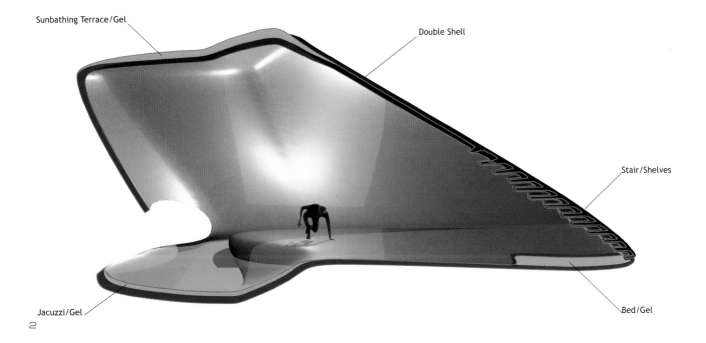

Sunbathing Terrace/Gel

Double Shell

Stair/Shelves

Jacuzzi/Gel

Bed/Gel

2

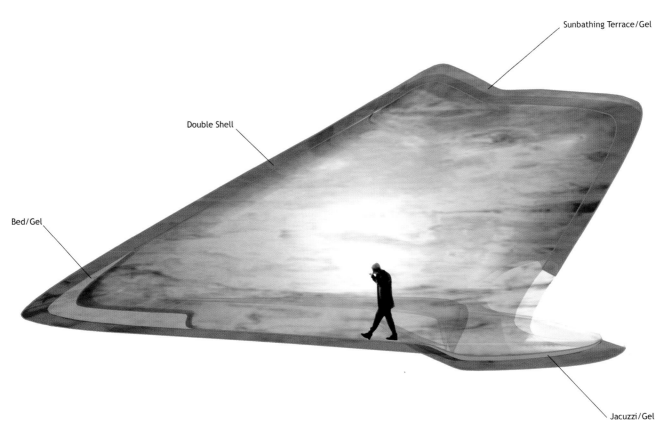

Sunbathing Terrace/Gel

Double Shell

Bed/Gel

Jacuzzi/Gel

3

OCEAN UK

OCEAN MEMBRANE

Technology

Three classes of prestressed polycarbonate tube extrusion can potentially be mass-produced on any scale. All the systems can extend infinitely, as the standard units are joined with concealed male/female pin joints. The structural fields operate interdependently as the three systems intertwine excessively, achieving structural stability while maintaining continuous dynamism.

Contextual Data

The generic structural systems interact with numerous dynamic conditions of tidal (downwells, upwells, rip tides, near-field waves, far-field waves, wave diffractions and refractions, and so on) and wind forces (laminar, strata, turbulent coastal interaction, and so on). The context, which is assumed to be a tidal estuary on an unnamed South Pacific island, provides a challenging environment in which to achieve the goals set out by the Shoreline Membrane Design Competition organizing committee.

Potential applications

The technological experiment has manifold potential programmatic implications for construction over, on, and under water in a range of contexts:

- industrial—water separation for fisheries and for desalination plants
- infrastructural—a bridge/tunnel
- leisure—fresh-water pools, climate-controlled pools in salt/cool water.

Implications

The project is intended to fall between known categories of bridge and tunnel. It offers an intermediate proposal, between the specific and the general, as an interface, modulated by contextual flows. The membrane does not separate exterior and interior, but opens an osmotic medium whose operation depends on the material conditions of the structural system rather than formal or optical shapes. The form of this entry results from the dynamic material performance of polycarbonate tubing on two scales, and reinforced resin meshes, rather than the traditional opposition of inside–outside.

1 Ocean membrane plan: estuary

2 Axonometric

3 Integration of all tectonic systems at one instant

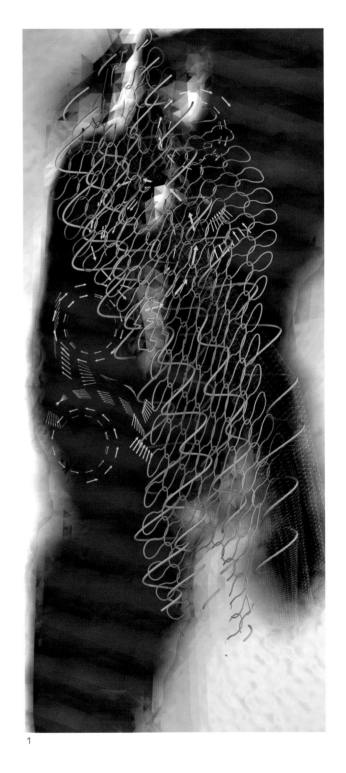

1

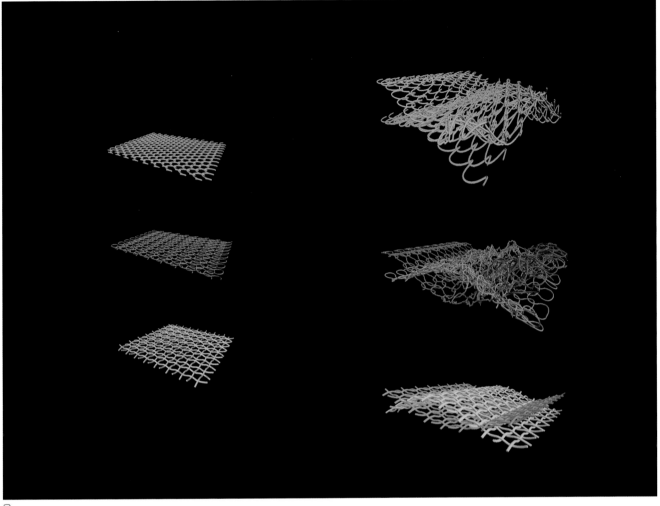

2

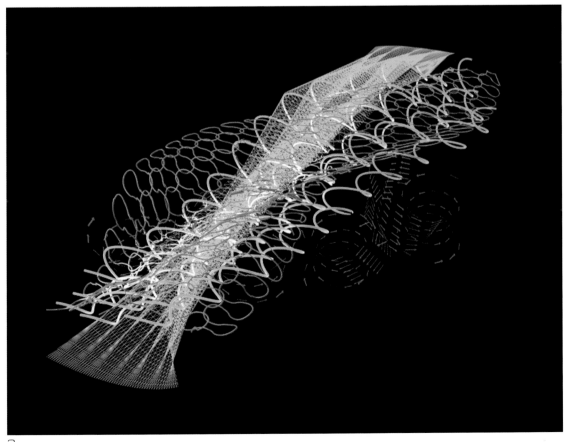

3

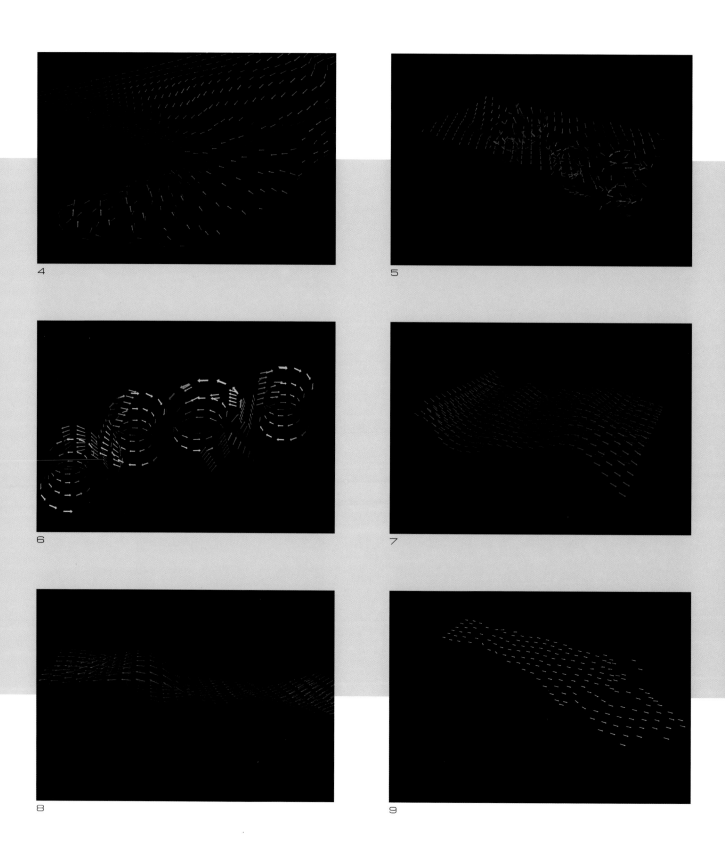

4

5

6

7

8

9

CYBER**SPACE**

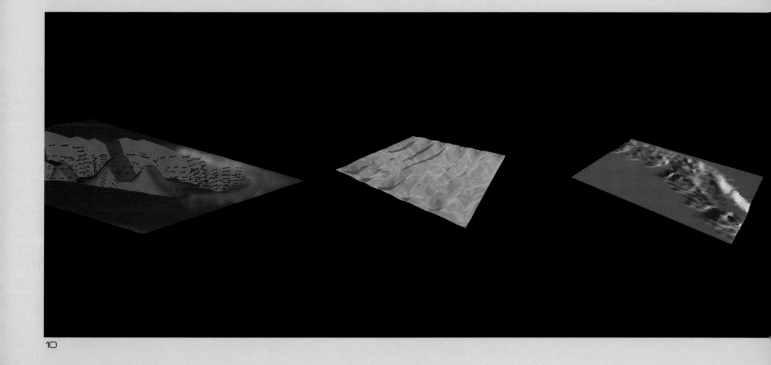

10

SHUBIN + DONALDSON

OGILVY & MATHER ADVERTISING AGENCY

Ogilvy & Mather is an award-winning advertising agency with clients that include American Express, Ford Motor Company, and Jaguar.

The site is the interior of an existing warehouse in Culver City. The entry is through a glass wall, cut out of the existing building. A 40-foot-long aluminum-clad tunnel, lit from below, leads the user from the entry into the work areas. Large plexiglass walls, overlaid with colorful images, divide production areas. The procession ends at the main conference room, carved out of the existing slab, and surrounded by 20-foot-high glass walls.

1

2

1 Digital rendering of interior
2 Digital rendering of entry
3 Digital rendering of reception desk
4 Digital rendering of exterior

SHUBIN + DONALDSON

OCEAN UK AND OCEAN US

OPERATION [INTERFACE]

Space

The horizontal surfaces of the Canadian Centre for Architecture (CCA) and the Espace Callot à l'Institute Français d'Architecture (IFA) are mediated and transformed by pliant, parallel topographies. The ambition is to construct spatial interiors that are the products of two intersecting surfaces. A clear diagram evolves from parallel configurations towards intersectional conditions of enclosure.

Physical Sites

The two intersecting surfaces are designed as modulations within a potentially extensive series of transformations. The physical sites are proposed as frozen moments in the shifting configurations of the two surfaces, scaled to be contextualized to the sites.

Technology

The spaces are co-configured as the intersections of divergent and convergent surfaces that cross and separate. The two physical installations are constructed from a standard unit of polycarbonate sheets, of 20:1 proportion, with a thickness of 20 millimeters. The concept is lightweight and low-risk for loading on floor surfaces. The polycarbonate sheets alternate at the inflections to form stiff junctions, where load is transferred to the floor/ground. The sheets are connected with extruded composite dowels, impregnated with fiber-optic strands. Both the sheets and the dowels are to be 50 percent translucent material, acting as a light-reflecting and absorbing surface for Solotech projections.

Effects

A continuous envelope inscribes the sectional space of a new, mobile ground, causing a heightened experience of visual, spatial, and gravitational instability. The supple intersections are in constant dynamic flux. The visual porosity of the installation fluctuates between two conditions: one of translucence and projected light reflection; and one of a transparent filtering of views and light, caused by the 20 millimeter spacings between polycarbonate slabs. Solotech multimedia projections will be installed above and below, indulging in the translucent effects.

1 Surface topography of laminated surfaces of installation

2 Elevation of intersecting surfaces

3 Plan of installation at CCA

1

2

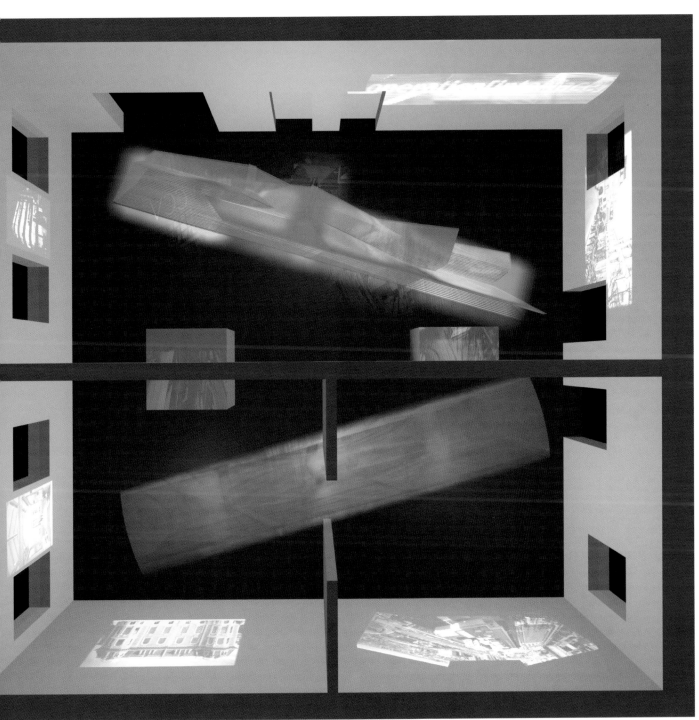

3

4

4 View of installation at CCA

5 Plan of installation at IFA

6 View of installation at IFA

CYBER**SPACE**

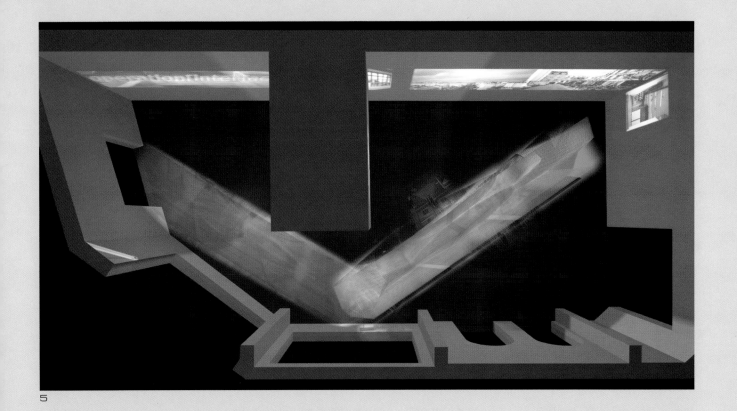

5

6

MARK BURRY
& GRANT DUNLOP

Between Surface and Substance

A paramorph is a body that may change its form while maintaining its basic properties or characteristics. Two paramorphs may appear different, but are fundamentally the same, their chemical or geometric principles sharing a common foundation.

The term 'paramorph' is taken from geology, and within this field is used to describe a mineral that derives from another, and has the same chemical composition. A paramorph, therefore, in the architectural context, refers to an object or artifact (that is, the digital parametric model) which, while maintaining the same internal structure or composition (that is, the explicit description of the geometry or topology of the model), is able to accommodate or adapt to a variety of physical forms or representations.

In the context of this exercise, the process of 'paramorphosis' consists of the transformation of what we term the 'dumb box', or the neutral starting point of the model, into one of the more highly articulated forms of the later stages of the exercise.

The paramorph is a curious mixture of both unstable and stable characteristics. The explicit and exacting description of the geometry of the various elements of the paramorph forms the stable component. The subentities of the model, their parameters, and the relationships between the various subentities, are described in a very formal manner, without scope for ambiguity or uncertainty. The resultant unstable objects and surfaces that can be generated from this stable description offer an endless scope for formal and spatial exploration and experimentation.

The paramorph is simultaneously able to contain qualities both of the stable and the unstable. Providing a framework in which the current desire for formal expression may be explored, it provides a language through which such forms and spaces may be explored, and more importantly, may be captured or represented. This is the necessary mediating step through which such forms may be realized through physical means and materials.

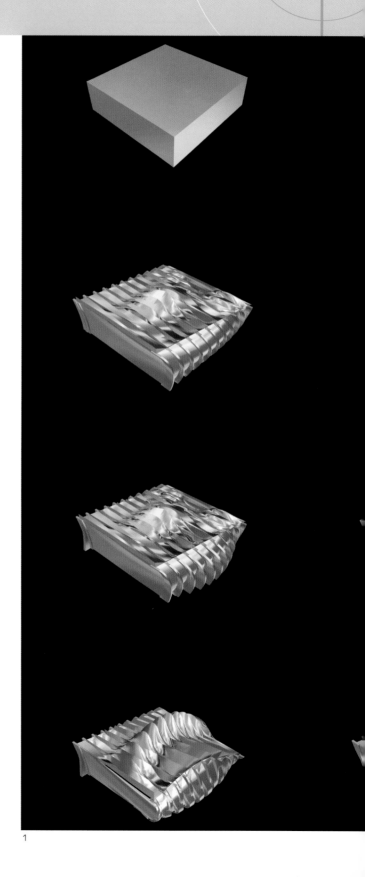

1

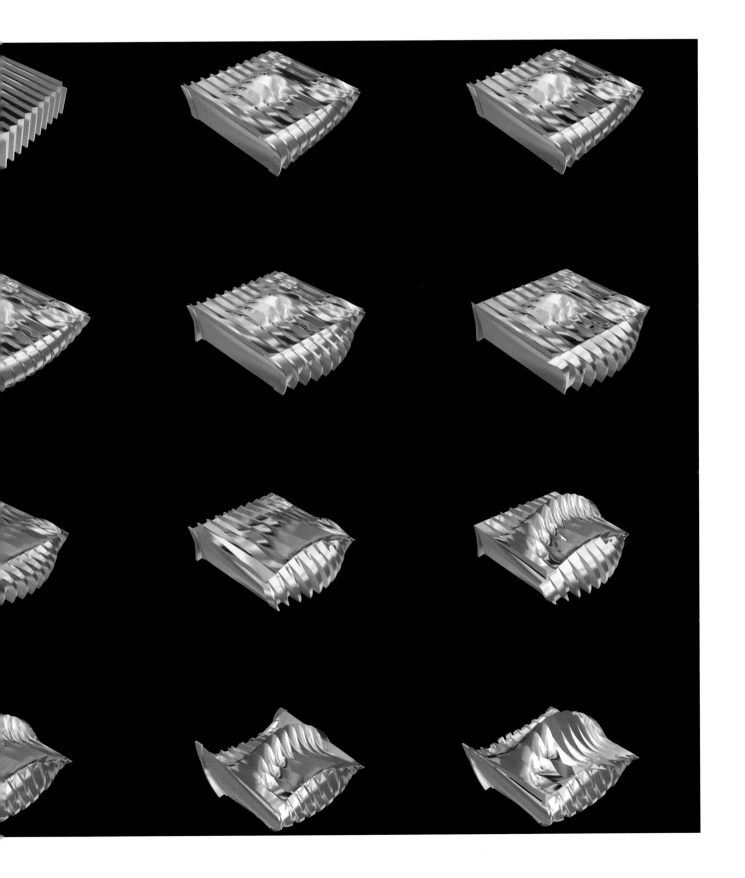

MARK BURRY & GRANT DUNLOP

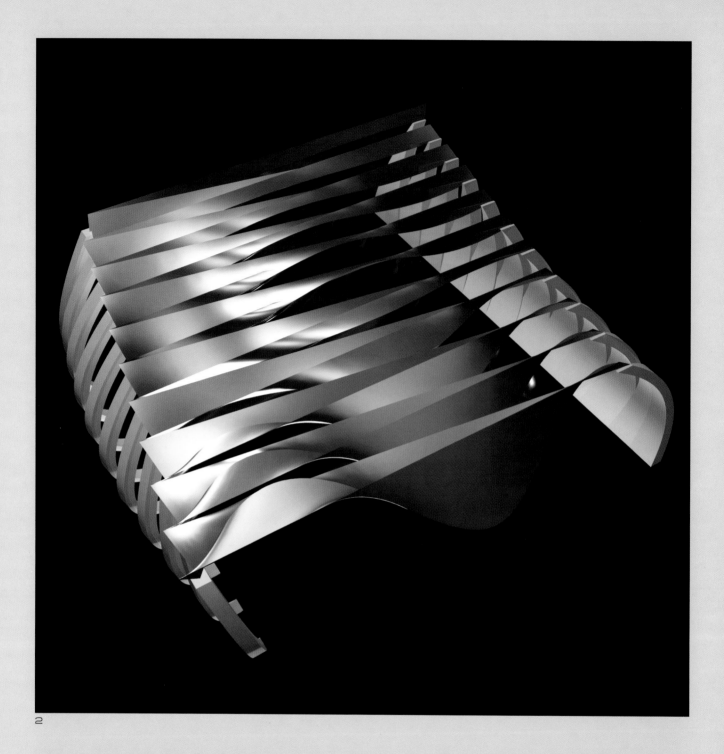

2

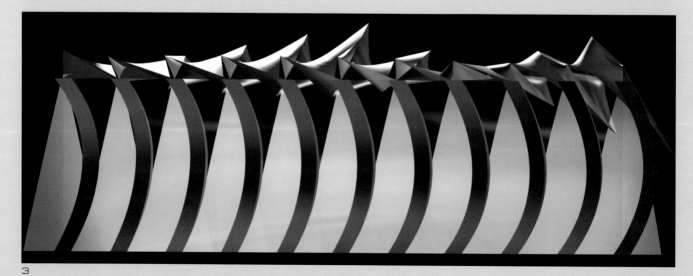

3

4

5

MARK BURRY **& GRANT DUNLOP**

dECOi/
DEAKIN UNIVERSITY

PARAMORPH II

The Paramorph II project has been developed for an architectural/art competition to devise a 'gateway' to the cultural centre of the South Bank in London, specifically for a passageway beneath the viaduct between the Eurostar terminal of Waterloo and esplanade, which houses the Royal Festival Hall, the National Theatre, the British Film Institute, the Queen Elizabeth Hall, and so on.

It is part of a major redevelopment of the area, and aims to stimulate what has been a quite dilapidated area behind Britain's major cultural institutions. The form is a series of curvilinear planes, a sort of vortex that negotiates between the scale of the plaza of Sutton Place, accelerating as it folds down into the constrained space of Sutton Passage: a gateway in depth and in movement.

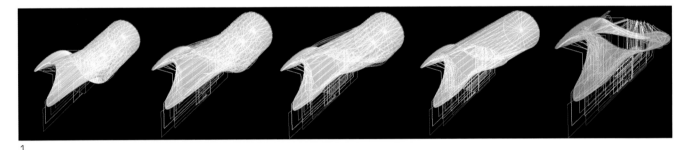

1

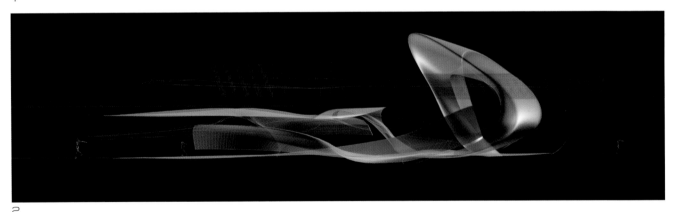

2

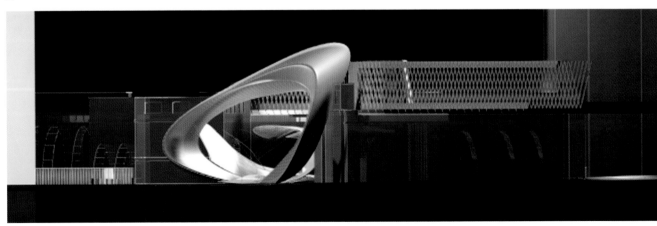

3

1 Paramorphosis: sequential relaxing of
  'parametric tube'

2 Sectional view of final design

3 Sutton Place elevation of final design

4 Plan view of final design

5 Concert hall elevation of final design

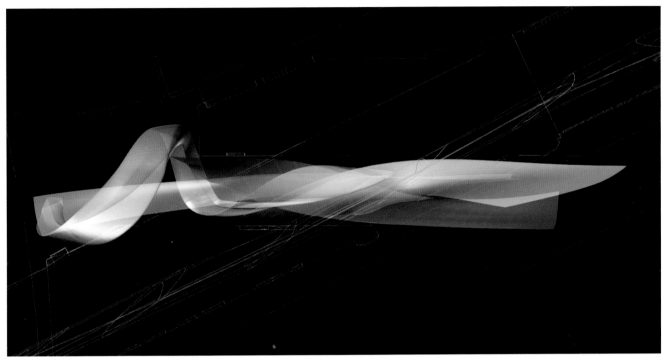

4

5

The Raybould House is located in Connecticut, USA, on 5.5 acres of partly wooded land. There are several existing structures on the property, namely a pool, a barn, and a traditional 'saltbox'-type house. A small creek runs over the length of the property. The project will be designed and built in several phases, including landscaping, the renovation of the barn, and a pool house. The new house, connecting to the existing salt-box, constitutes Phase 1.

The new house is a chimera, an organic hybrid. It takes its cues from the logics of the traditional house and the landscape respectively. Unlike other kinds of hybrids, the chimera constitutes a new functional *and* structural unity. Consequently, the new house has a formal, structural, and systemic identity all its own, suggesting uncanny properties beyond the repertory of known ones.

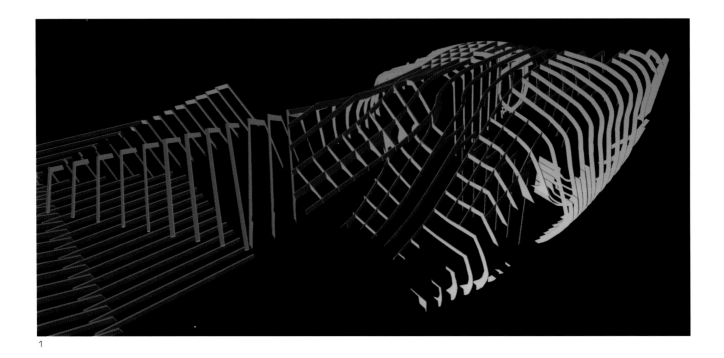

1

1 Plywood rib configuration for base of shell showing transformation of rafter to inverted hull
2 North view showing both stacked bedrooms including separate entries from terrace and exterior stair; upper living room and terrace is at rear
3 Entry to lower living level with terrace

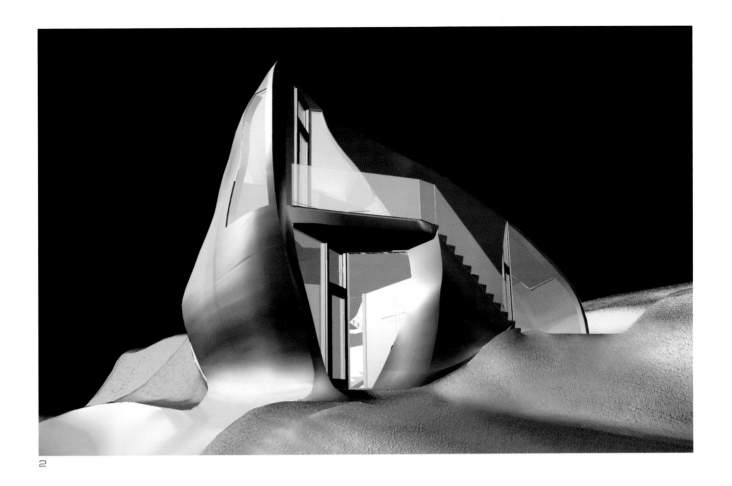

2

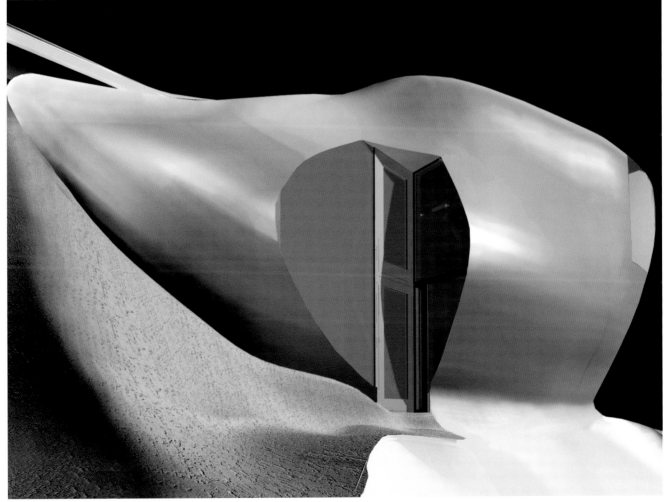

3

4

5

6

4 Roof plan

5 Overall east view

6 South view at entry to bridge

7 Lower level plan including upper and lower
living rooms and daughter's bedroom/bath

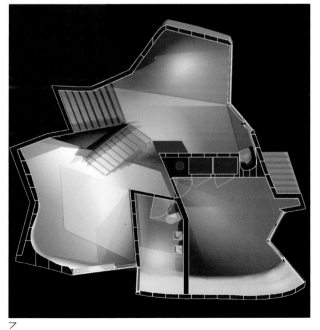

7

8 Section through bridge and lower and upper living rooms

9 Section through lower living room and both bedrooms

10 Upper level plan including master bedroom, bathroom, upper and lower level living rooms

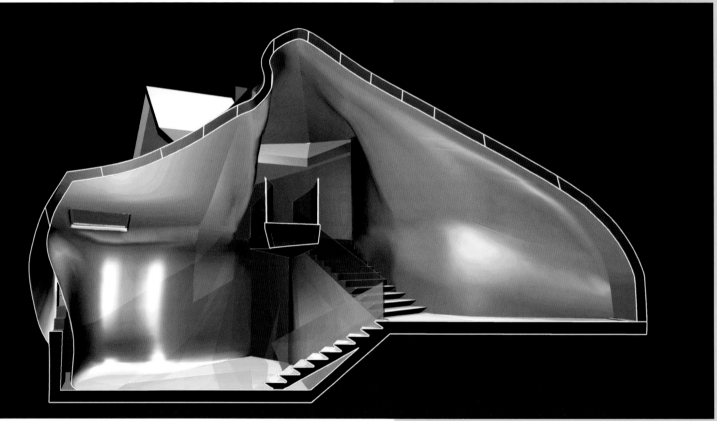

8

9

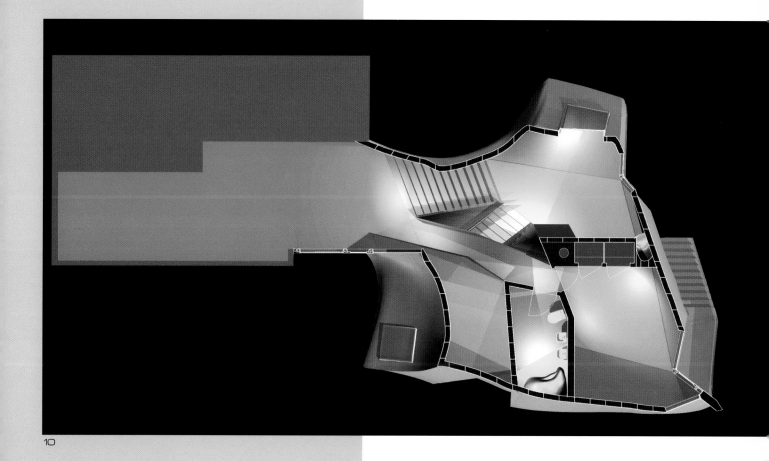

10

KOLATAN/ MAC DONALD STUDIO

RESI-RISE SKYSCRAPER

The Resi-Rise is less building, more 'vertical urbanism'. Its frame, not unlike a spatial matrix of 'lots', is initially built out to the maximum allowable zoning envelope, with deformations accounting for site influences such as views and adjacencies.

Once the territory is staked out, the frame is ready for rental space in the form of pods. It is possible for individual tenants to inhabit their spaces without depending on the full occupation of the building itself. Assuming that the top and bottom are considered 'most desirable', the Resi-Rise can already be operational as it fills up from top and bottom first, leaving the mid-section free to be taken later. Following the urban analogy, this would be much like

being among the first to live on a new block with the necessary infrastructure in place, but unlike residing in a partially populated shell-and-core building.

The morphology, size, program, function, materials, servicing, and furnishing of the pods are customizable within parameters set by the architects. This strategy couples individual choice (via the development of mass-customized units) with the collective performance and identity of the Resi-Rise to form a complex system of relations between the whole and its parts. Individual residents can play a role in the spatial organization of their pods into contiguous or distributed affiliations of space. When tenants leave, old pods are removed and recycled. Within this structure, it becomes feasible for short-term

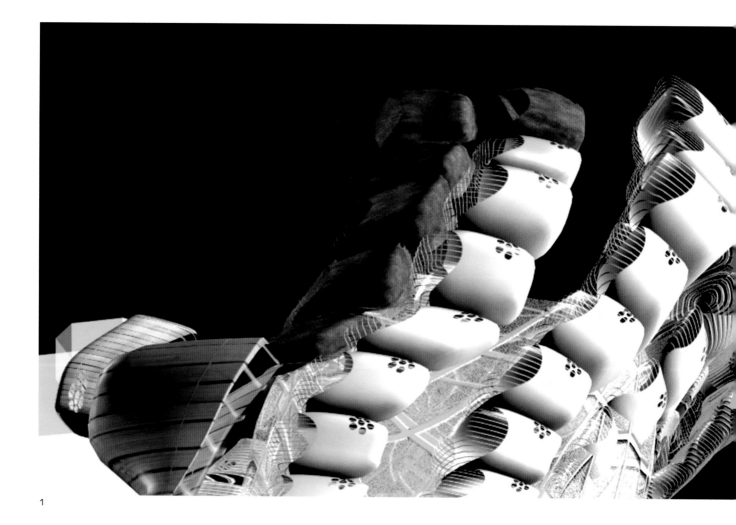

1

1 Detail view of top

2 Overall view looking west along 57th Street

3 Detail view of mid-rise section including cinema

4 Detail view of low-rise section

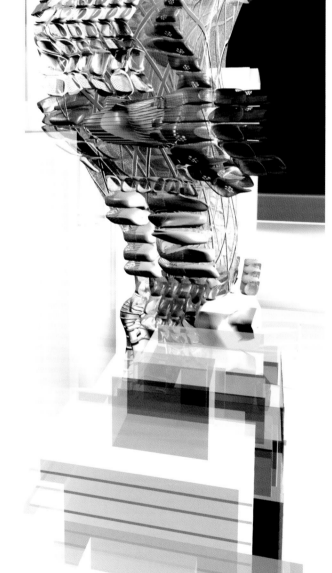

2

3

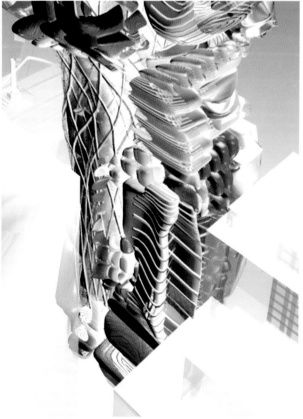

4

KOLATAN/MAC DONALD **STUDIO**

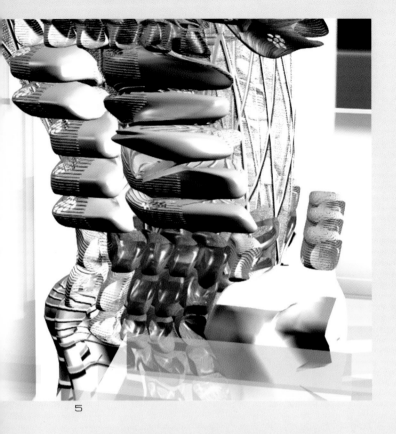

5

6

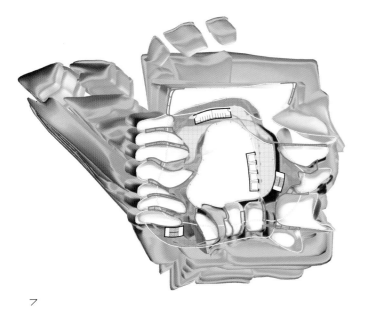

7

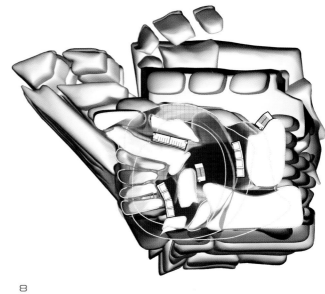

8

9

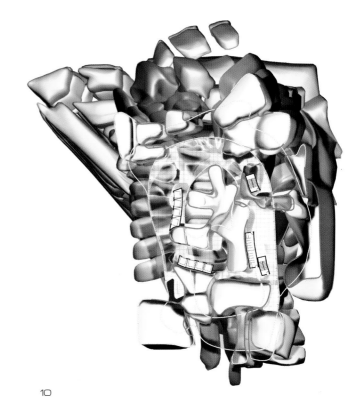

10

programmatic scenarios, such as corporate leasing of space for the duration of a convention for instance, to come (and go) with their own pods.

The pod is less like real estate and more like a leased car to the tenant. In this proposal the architects continue to remain involved with their 'product' by updating it as new materials and technologies emerge onto the market. This gives the owner/tenant the option to upgrade to the latest model, but due to

the continuing development of accessories for use in conjunction with the pods, and the supply to the user of information on compatible third-party products, the construction of the Resi-Rise is never quite finished.

KOLATAN/MAC DONALD **STUDIO**

OOSTERHUIS.NL

SALT WATER PAVILION

The Salt Water Pavilion is the first true 'body' building to display real-time behavior. The body is generated in the weightless digital realm and is embedded in an artificial island on Earth. The Salt Water Pavilion captures raw data from a weather station on a buoy in the sea, and transcribes the data into an emotional factor. The black body of the Salt Water Pavilion feeds on data. Inside the black body, the lights are continuously changing in real-time—visitors feel themselves immersed in the dynamic light and sound massage.

1 Body scans are thin slices of the three-dimensional model; they facilitate communication between building partners

2 The body juts out 12 meters over the oosterschelde; the robust contruction resists the stormy sea

3 Unibody conceived as fusion of metal and concrete; public follows three-dimensional folded moebius trajectory

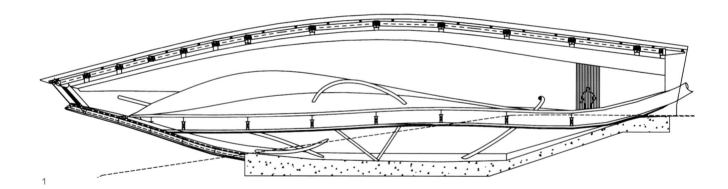

1

2

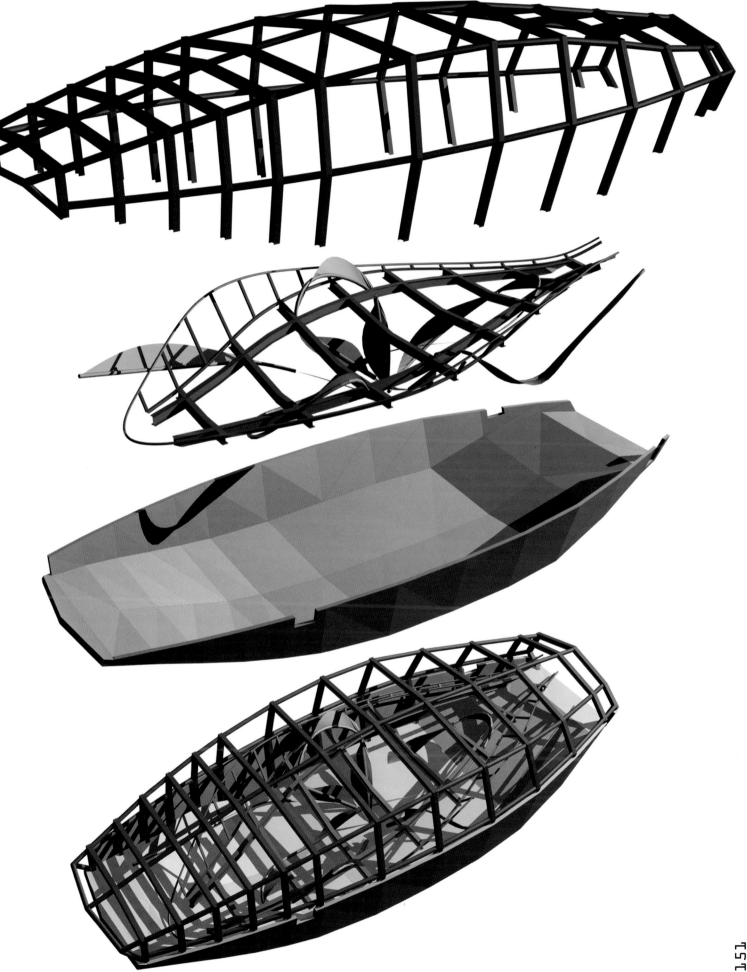

4 The hydra, wrapped in transparent green elastic latex, has dynamically programmable effects which accompany visitors along their trajectory

5 The 100-meter, curved hydra supports the wavefloor and connects the underwater 'wetlab' with the sensorium

6 Self-contained unibody transported by sea and assembled on site: X-ray vision of wetlab and sensorium

7 Visitors influence the sensorium light and sound environment; sound samples generate the sound in real-time

4

5

6

7

AMMAR ELOUEINI, DIGIT-ALL STUDIO

SARAJEVO CONCERT HALL

Metastasis

This project, for the Sarajevo Concert Hall Competition, was approached in relation to a dilemma between the context and the program. The context is very poor but emblematic at the same time. Being in the midst of a newly planned urban zone makes the Concert Hall one of the most significant buildings in this area. The Concert Hall's relationship to the history of this region and its very deep connection to music make it a very important building in a period of reconstruction after several years of civil war.

Double-Membrane

The Concert Hall was first modeled as a double membrane on the site. The inner membrane retraces different musical tempos, and the outer membrane retraces the city's vibrations, noises, and breath.

Using computer techniques, animations simulating a double system of reaction between the membranes and sound input were produced. The two membranes were modeled as being very close to one another. An interstitial space was created as a result of the reactions of both membranes.

The second phase of the design process consisted of recreating the double-membrane system for each programmatic element. Each part of the program was modeled with a different interior/exterior sound input. The general behavior of the double-membrane system, and the local variations of each of the components, determined spaces, which could then be modified and altered in relation to local variations and global behavior.

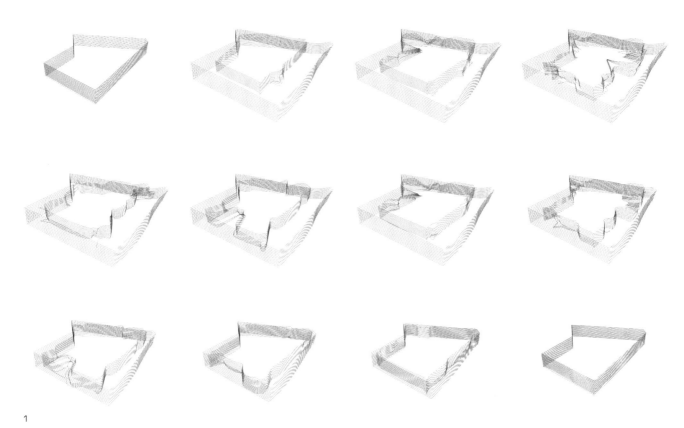

1

154

1 Stills from animation, showing interaction
between the two membranes
2 Building structure

2

AMMAR ELOUEINI, **DIGIT-ALL STUDIO**

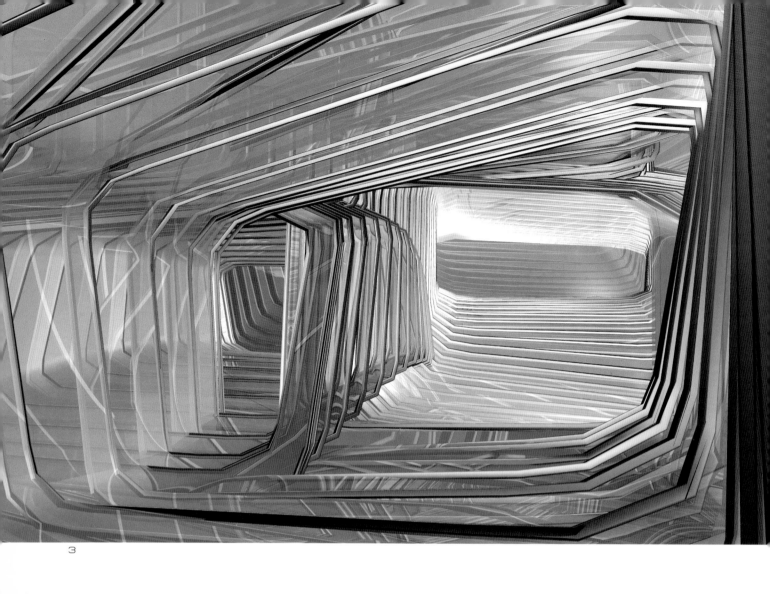

3

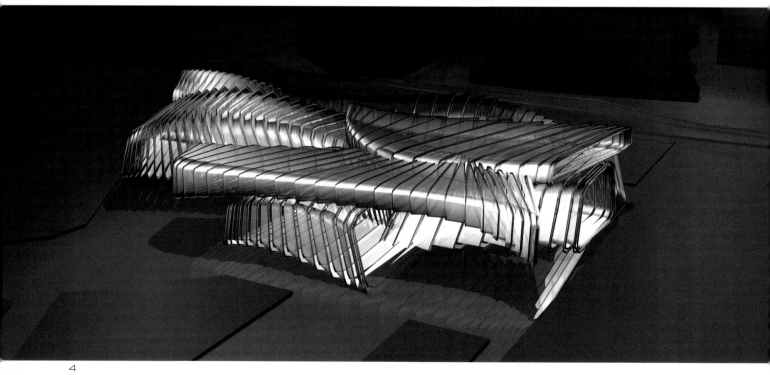

4

CYBER**SPACE**

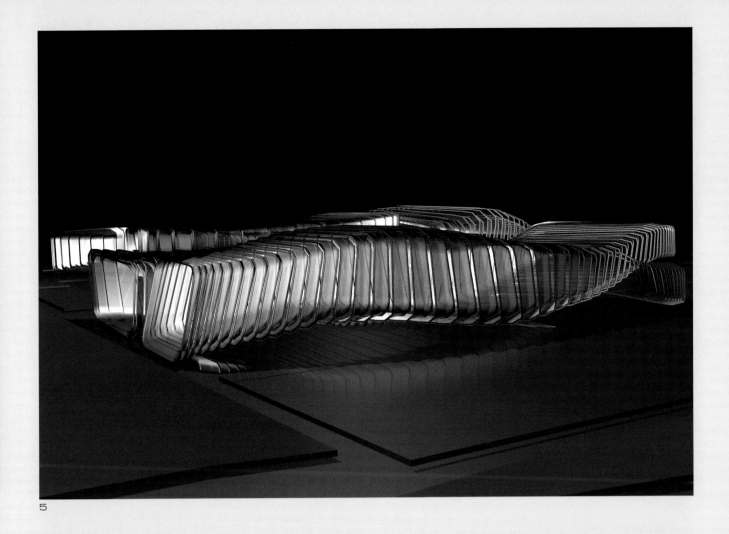

5

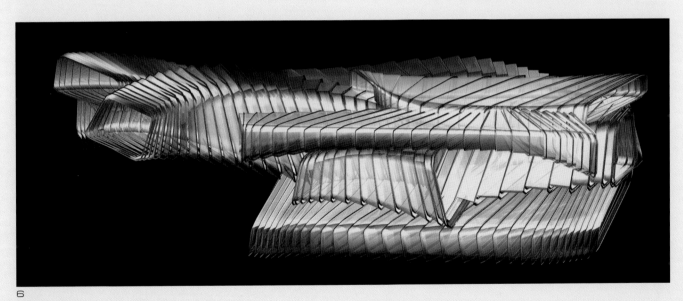

6

3 Interior view at junction of rehearsal and
administration areas

4 View of Concert Hall towards the city
center

5 Main entrance and cafeteria

6 General view of Concert Hall

ALSOP & STÖRMER

Alsop & Störmer wished to find a new use for a listed silo in Rotterdam, which was coming to the end of its life. The structure was very dense and strong, and was designed to withstand explosions within the silo.

The building is located in the southern part of the inner city by the water. As part of the analysis, the firm examined the future of this part of the city for living as well as pleasure.

This project was explored in terms of function, context, and finance, and the solution found was that the program of spaces would be determined by what was possible to easily remove.

The result of this exercise suggested that the space was suited to performance, and even while empty, the space itself was always giving a 'spatial opera.' The silo was therefore renamed The Opera House.

1   Cloudy environment
2   Transparent silo
3   Spiral transporter

1

2

3

SHUBIN + DONALDSON

SOUND STUDIO

The multi-dimensional wall forms corridors and creates new space as it finds its way through the elongated office. The strange curves appear to be responding to a frozen sound wave that has cut through the rational grid of recycled paper panels. The space and form dance together, tethered in contrast. The shape is a lost echo from a distant source, captured and held in place by a rigid steel frame.

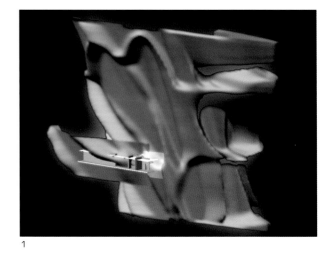

1

1   Digital conceptual visualization
2&3   Digital rendering of interior
4&5   Digital rendering of entry

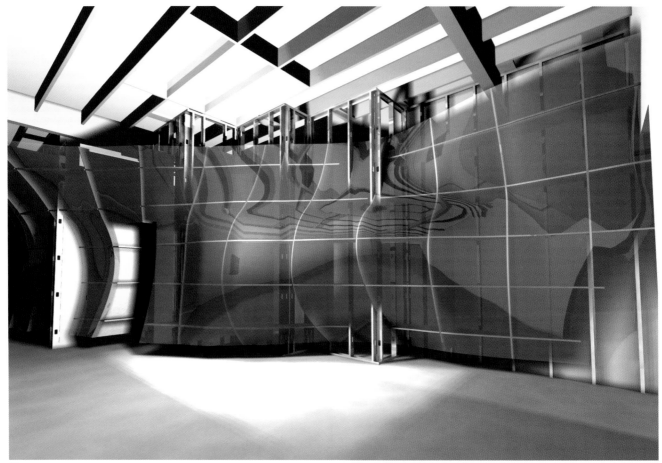

2

3

4

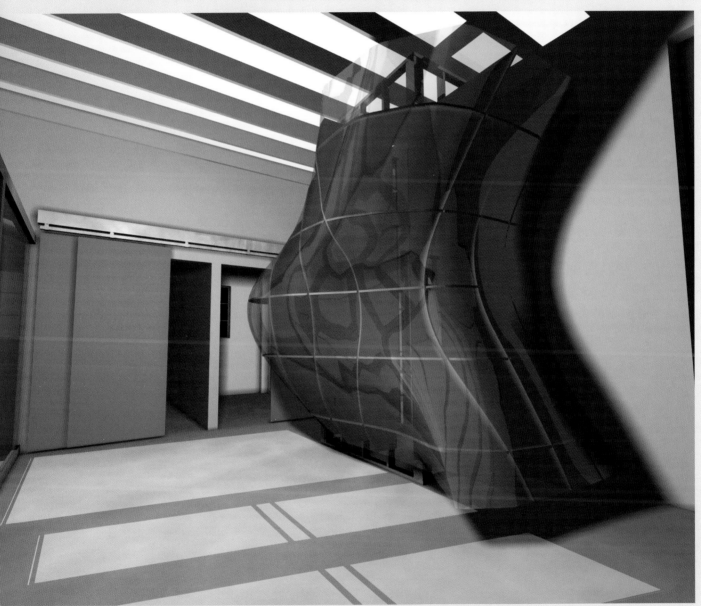

5

DR HARESH LALVANI

Spheroids is best suited for a cluster of large-scale but freely connected spaces and flexible layouts on multiple levels as in a museum, convention hall, cultural center, a pavilion at a world fair, or a greenhouse. The varying tilts, heights, and curvature of the ellipsoidal vaults accentuate each space differently. The transparent, vaulted spaces can be proportioned individually for specific functions, and can be added or removed to make larger or smaller clusters according to program requirements. Spheroids is composed of intersecting prolate and oblate ellipsoids projected from six-dimensional Euclidean space, and can be easily manipulated in cyberspace where a suitable design configuration can be selected from the infinite compositional possibilities in three-dimensional space (see pages 36–7).

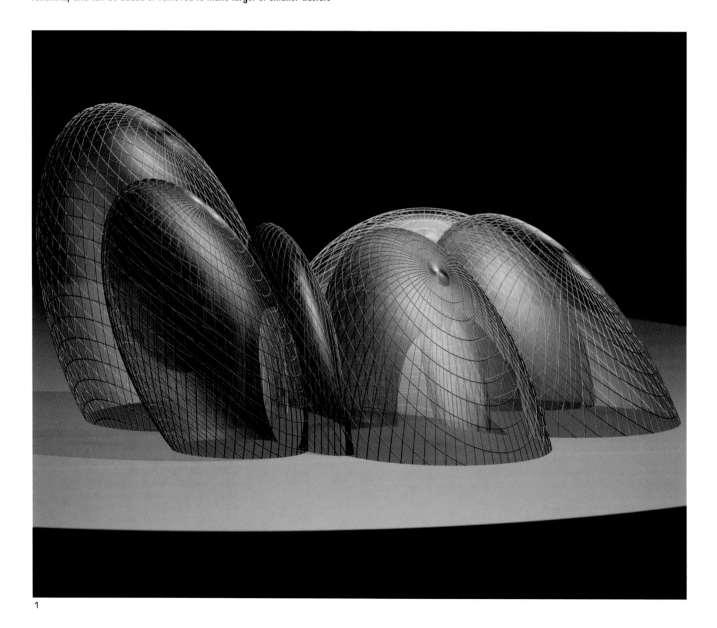

1

2

1 Exterior view

2 Interior view

DR HARESH **LALVANI**

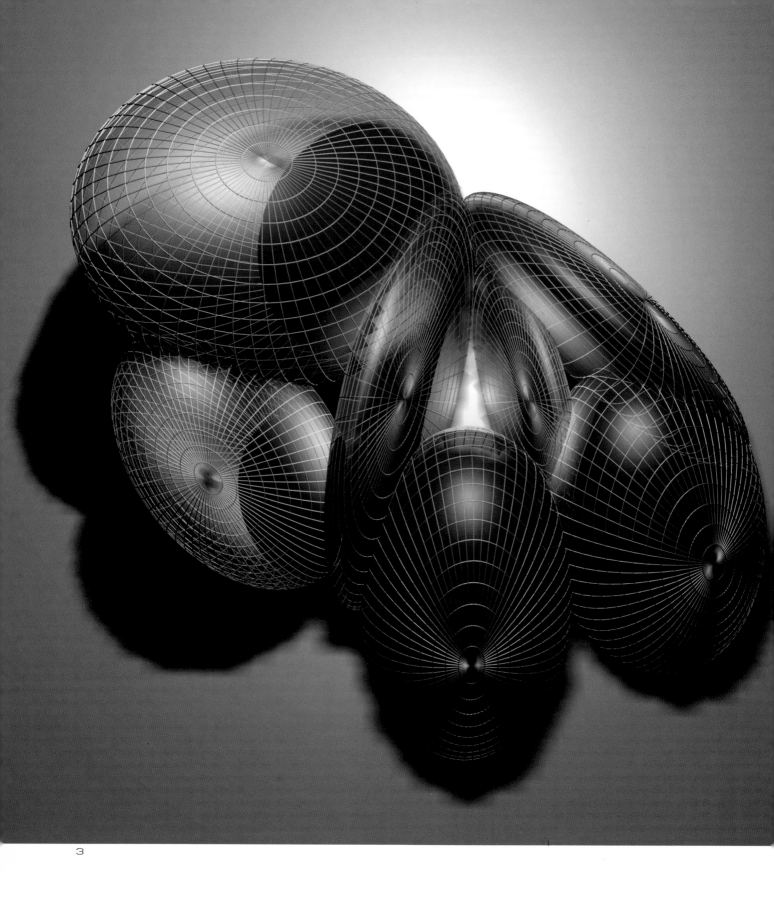

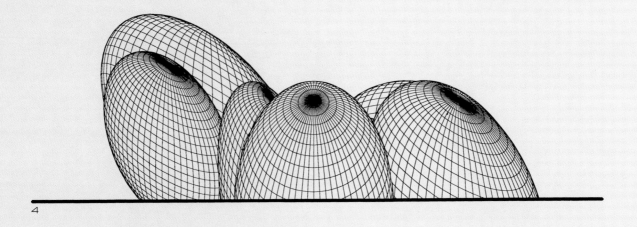

4

5

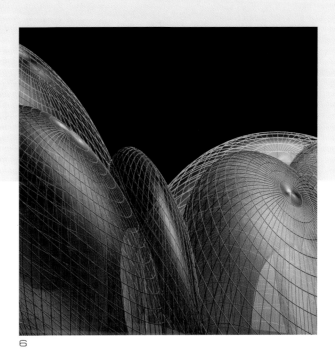

6

3 Plan view

4 Elevation view

5 Close-up, plan view

6 Close-up, exterior view

DR HARESH **LALVANI**

ARCHI-TECTONICS

STRATEGIC (RE)OCCUPATIONS

Due to its geopolitical location in the New York Bay, Governors' Island has functioned mainly as a military outpost for Manhattan. As a result, the island is not subject to New York City law but rather to New York State law. Since the Second World War, it has been occupied by the Coast Guard.

The constantly fluctuating geographical shape of the island was fixed in 1912 when it was extended with soil excavated from subway constructions. It therefore consists of an old part, with the New York bedrock, and a new part that has been artificially reclaimed. Spring tides still flood the island and occasionally threaten its existence.

The Coast Guard is currently in the process of leaving, freeing up the island for new use. The old part is occupied by the original structures, which will be designated 'Landmarks in the Park'. The newer, reclaimed section has no real urban or architectural value—a hybrid surface, an existing infrastructure deserted.

The island is a *tabula rasa*. A new law will have to be developed, with new codes and coordinates. It will be necessary to analyze traces, develop a new strategy, map out new possibilities and occupations. What is the future of an island so close to the metropolis? How does one develop an occupation pattern? Here migration replaces stability, producing new settlements.

The inherent memory of the island constitutes a permanently unstable entity, a constantly evolving structure. The introduction of pier structures on the west side will cause a gradual settlement of sand particles along that boundary, and the growth of a naturally protected beach. The piers will also provide the foundations for future housing structures, temporal dwellings, balancing on the edge of the stable and unstable regions.

The apartments will form horizontal bands of private space, twisting around and over the piers—the public space—thus intertwining and dissolving the boundaries between the public and the private. The reclaimed sector of the island will contain services such as sports facilities, shops, restaurants, cinema, and public green spaces for the new residents.

1

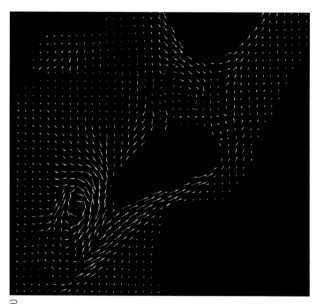

2

1　Pier and apartment structures

2　Turbulence diagram of water currents around island

3　Perspective from Manhattan

4　Proposed island 'growth' diagram, through introduction of piers

5　Overview

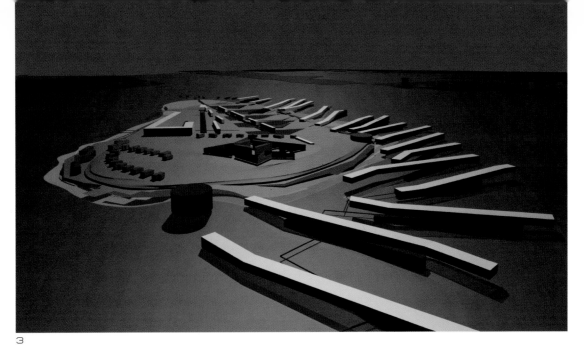

3

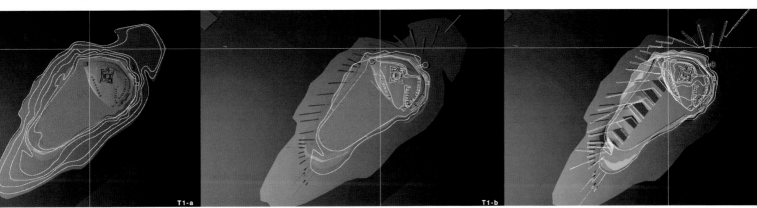

T1-a   T1-b

4

5

Also in Raissa, city of sadness, there runs an invisible thread that binds one living being to another for a moment, then unravels, then is stretched again between moving points as it draws new and rapid patterns so that every second the unhappy city contains a happy city unaware of its own existence.

Italo Calvino—*Invisible Cities*

With the privatization of energy companies, a positive public image is a requisite for success. As a focus of contemporary design inquiry, the representation of the power plant in the landscape, and the consequent implied character of its products (and byproducts), raises issues both portentous and timely, as well as ideological and ethical, regarding architectural camouflage, (in)congruity with context, and the nature of nature.

Program
The client, Sunlaw Energy Corporation, has invested in developing clean-energy sources to convert natural gas to electricity. It is also interested in not pretending to be something other than what it is. At the same time, the leadership of the company is enlightened and socially conscious enough to understand the imperative to discreetly cloak itself without trying to disguise itself as an over-scaled bucolic barn or simulated tree.

Zoning Constraints
The existing power plant meets industrial zoning requirements for the site. Design constraints for the power plant require a minimum stack height of 130 feet, access to the plant engine, and 50 percent opacity of the structural canopy for adequate ventilation.

Location
Sunlaw retained Moore Ruble Yudell to design a prototype canopy and enclosure for their case study power plant in a mixed residential–industrial neighborhood in Los Angeles.

1   View from freeway
2   Lighting study of power plant stack

1

2

Process

Research tower precedents: visionary towers, towers in ancient history, the towers of Babel, towers as lighthouses, towers as energy sources (that is, windmills), towers as symbols, towers of information, air-traffic control towers, towers as markers (campaniles, city landmarks), towers as solar collectors, towers representing culture, minarets, spires, towers of light.

Solution

As an overall concept to unify the different parts of each plant unit, two formal schemes were merged to create the final design of the elliptical cylinder juxtaposed with the sweeping arc of steel canopy. This gesture acts to integrate the plant units' smokestacks with their power generators and scrubbers. The two plant units are juxtaposed and staggered, so that the silhouettes of two similar forms can be seen from the adjacent 710 freeway and from the surrounding streets. The skyline of the project formed by the curved and vertical elements provides a powerful symbol and landmark.

The design aspires to express the plant's function with an architecture that is honest, even celebratory, rather than attempting to disguise it, as has often been done elsewhere. To accentuate the visibility and reinforce the identity of the power plant, high technology has been used, involving machined materials such as steel and woven-wire mesh. Since ventilation is a major concern, the sweeping arc of the canopies will have less than 50 percent opacity. The design has many open elements throughout to accommodate the passage of air as well as for ease of maintenance of large pieces of equipment. All the sides as well as the top of the structure have openings. The plan for the building is also splayed, to reduce the massive appearance of the structure.

The elliptical cylinders containing the stacks are poised at an angle, giving these towers an active silhouette against the sky. A computerized lighting system animates the leaning towers, heralding the changes of seasons and events such as Halloween or the Fourth of July through the use of graphics and colors. Information about the environment and the use of energy sources can also be shown on the towers. The curved canopies reflect the distant mountain ranges surrounding the Los Angeles basin, while the rising towers evoke the dynamic imagery of Simon Rodia's famous nearby Watts Towers.

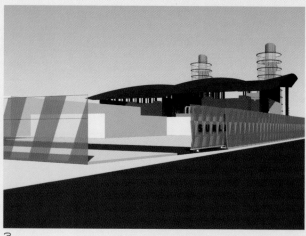

3

4

5

3 View from main entry

4 Night view

5 Process sketch layers three-dimensional model and drawing by hand

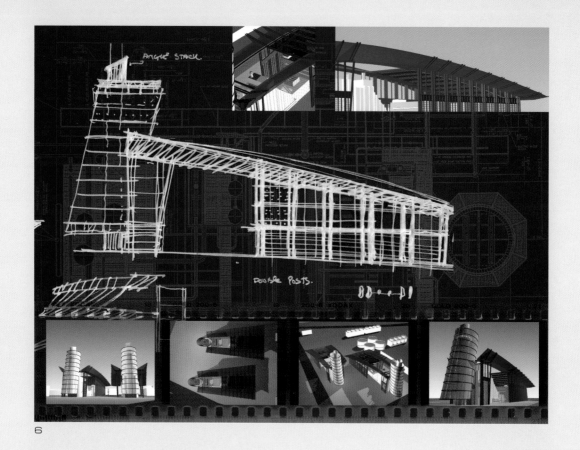

6

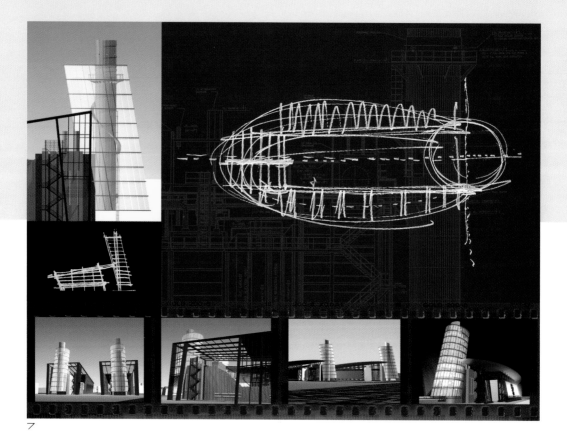

7

6-9 Three-dimensional form studies with
sketches

CYBER**SPACE**

8

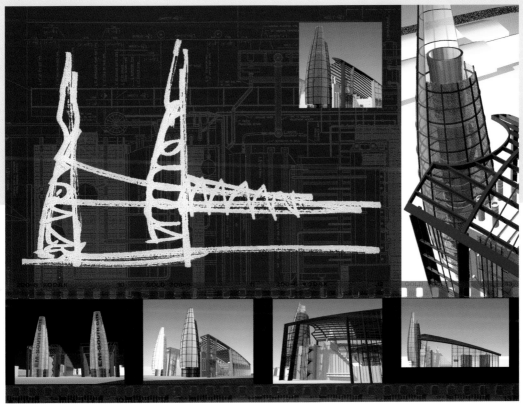

9

MICHAEL OSTWALD

TEMPORAL CIVIC ZONE

While architects and programmers are designing virtual workspaces to replace office buildings, and information super-highways to replace road and rail networks, the place of the town square seems to have been forgotten in the information age.

This project questions the capacity of civic spaces to exist in virtual environments. The Temporal Civic Zone is a storage vault that holds virtual reflections of a thousand of the world's key public places. These mirror sites are sensitively dependent on changes in their corresponding physical spaces.

Virtual visitors may log into the Temporal Civic Zone and search for signs of social interaction and responsibility around the world. When a physical site falls below a predetermined level of usage, its virtual reflection is deleted, leaving behind a permanent void in cyberspace.

1

2

3

1-4 Temporal Civic Zone

4

OOSTERHUIS.NL

THEATER DE WARANDE

In this architectural concept the auditorium feels like a solid rock in a sea of flow, amidst a stream of people always changing configuration. During performances the auditorium absorbs the fluid stream of the public—the architecture of the Theater de Warande is the embodiment of the process of flow.

The streamlined shape of the outer shell is folded around the program as an extra-large coat and by virtue of its inclining facades, space flows fluidly around the building body of the theater. The streamline respects the castle of the Dukes of Brabant, and leaves space for the tops of the old trees. The Theater de Warande is a vectorial body that communicates dynamics, flexibility, and openness.

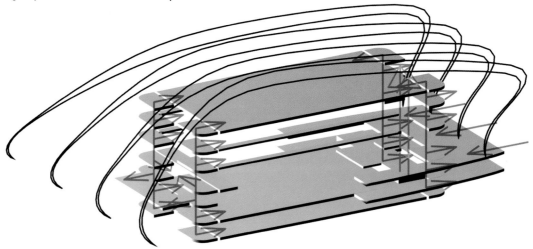

1

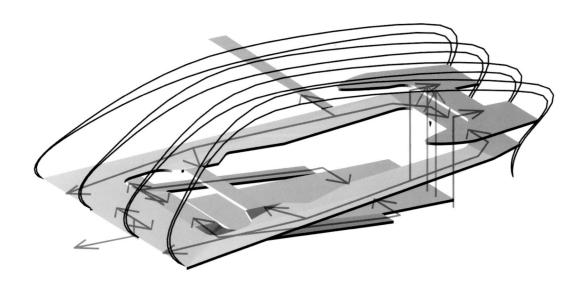

2

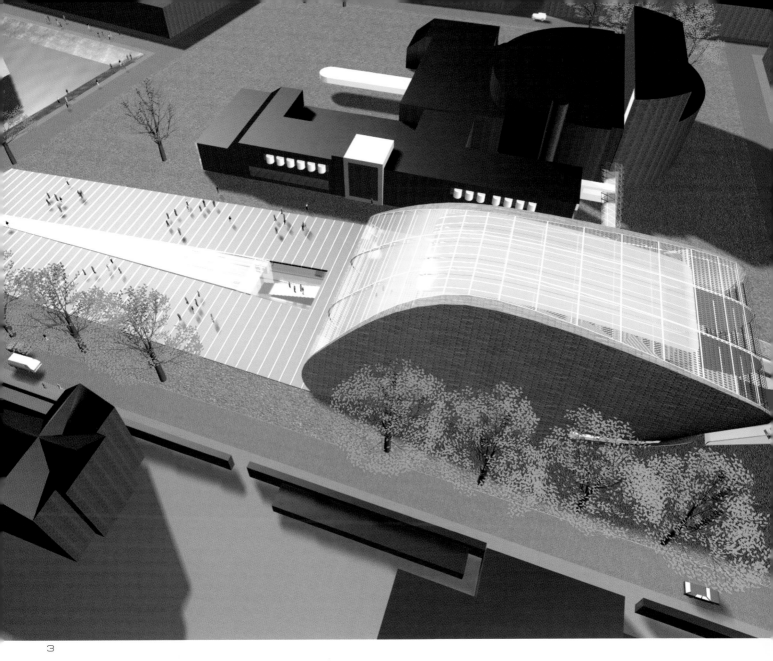

3

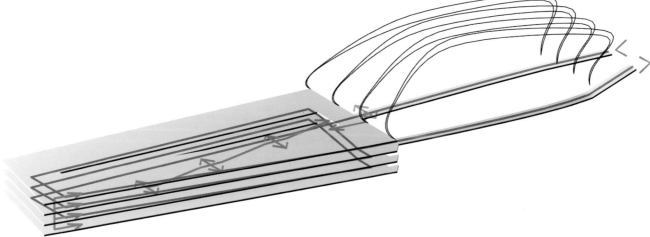

4

1 Circulation shortcuts around solid theater hall

2 Public circulation consists of gentle ramps

3 Body appears to move from square

4 Parking garage features spiral circulation concept

5

5 Exercise studios at end of ramp

6 Sloping transparent front and main
  entrance; circulation spaces connected
  to city

7 Sides are rich, textured, double-curved
  brick surfaces; technical curved glass roof
  with photovoltaic cells

8 Transparent entrance invites public to
  enter

9 Glass bridge connection with existing
  theater complex, it transforms elegantly
  from circular to oval shape

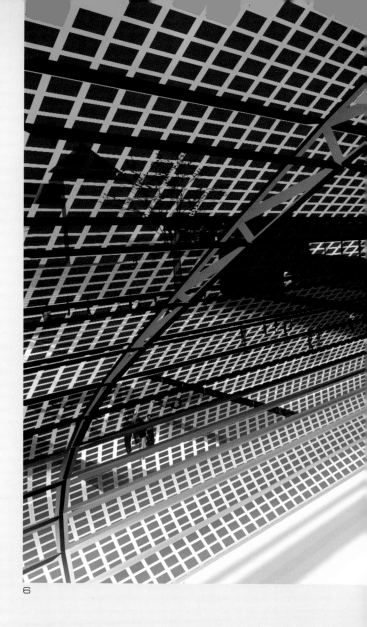

6

7

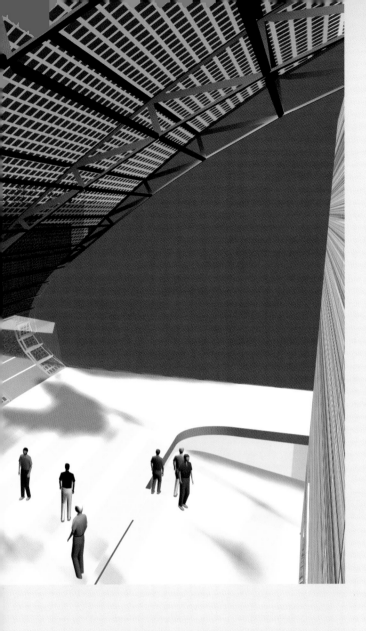

8

9

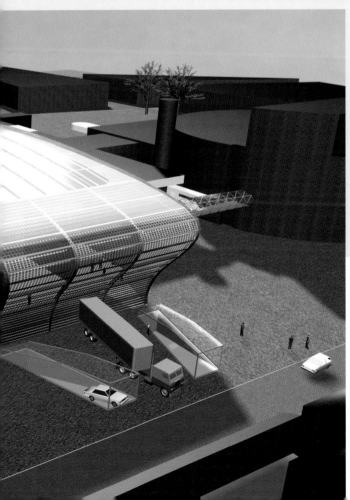

OCEAN UK AND OCEAN US

TIMES SQUARE DISCOUNT TICKETING CENTER

A Horizontal Times Square Ball

The design strategy respects an 11-foot height constraint and the need to avoid ground foundations. The result is a configuration of horizontal pedestrian flow patterns guided by orientation devices, and a multi-directional booth enclosure. It incorporates a ticket-purchasing system with a simple and effective assembly of elements in a technically innovative, durable, semipermanent structure. The visuality of the Times Square Ball has been presented in a lateral configuration, with equally stimulating and informative effects.

From Ground Movement to Enclosure

The scheme's micro-sectional configurations both 'ground' and 'figure' the urban surface, enhancing the structural stability of the booth volumes. The superstructure emerges from these 'micro-topographies', defining the accessibility and security of the ticketing booths. The membrane is generated from ribbons merged into a helical structure, and a loose, looped layer of fiber-optic cable between layers of corrugated skin made of a visually permeable polycarbonate. The diagonal intersection of seams takes on varying widths as it twists, each band overlapping the next for climate control.

Each section carries the flow of pedestrians perpendicular to the ground, with a minimum of interaction between the ground plane and the helical structure at one point. The adaptable, ribbon-like barricades orient a smooth pedestrian flow. The double helical structure of the membrane for the booth enclosures joins an applied second skin to the ground, creating a deck for the Visual Information Fountain (VIF) rods to slide on in tracks.

The VIFs are intersectional units that connect the continuous ribbon of pedestrian barricades to the ground. Each is a digital device designed to receive and emit visual information—projections, translucencies, and reflections—enabling the display of theater information on a smart skin of polycarbonate bands with information loops of fiber-optics embedded with networking hardware to transmit light and data. The VIFs will complement and enhance the LED and other screen technologies already existing in Times Square.

The queuing system maximizes pedestrian exposure to the ticketing booths. Depending on the time of day, the size of the queues can be varied to adapt to the requirements of the pedestrian flow.

1 Visual information fountains define site pedestrian movement
2 Corrugated polycarbonate ribbon enclosure
3 Horizontal pedestrian flow pattern

1

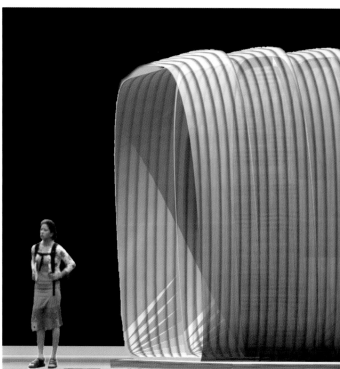

2

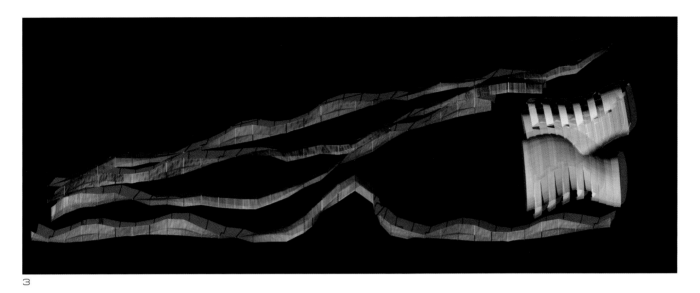

3

ARCHI-TECTONICS

TKTS—BOOTH AT TIMES SQUARE

The ticket booth as a hypersurface registers the flow pressures of Time Square's hyperactivity. This registration modulates the form in a 'soft architecture'. The 'soft booth' is a structure that has a suppleness in its positioning on the site, as well as in its integration of digital communication technology.

The layered, structural 'smart' skin envelopes not only the projection of information, but also provides lighting, cooling, and heating elements. Its aluminum reflective skin, reminiscent of the 1960s airstreams, does not imitate the 'super-sign', but instead creates a soft form that merely absorbs and reflects its surroundings. Simple, ever-changing text bands transmit logistic data on availability—software informs the 'soft booth'.

Inside, the booth creates an open field of activity: free-standing capsules (bathroom, wardrobe, storage), smart screens (information for salespeople and supervisor), and fluid work surfaces combine in an easygoing atmosphere with ultimate precision.

The 'soft booth' creates a ripple in the traffic island, with small paths defining an unforceful guidance of customers, possibly augmented with retractable skin-like partitions for 'top-sale' moments. The southern entrance is placed within the structural fold, which enables easy access for employees and messengers.

The exterior skin, malleable and reflective, is made of an aluminum composite material. It is constructed of prefabricated panels that sandwich plates of aluminum over a lightweight core made of metal mesh. This sleek, low-cost material is easily installed on site and is highly insulated—ideal for the functions of the 'soft booth'.

SECTION SHOWING LCD INFO SCREEN

WEST ELEVATION

TIMES SQUARE TICKET BOOTH C

1

2

1 Detail of structural skin of ticket booth
   with integrated animated text
2 View of supple integrated frame in
   aluminum skin

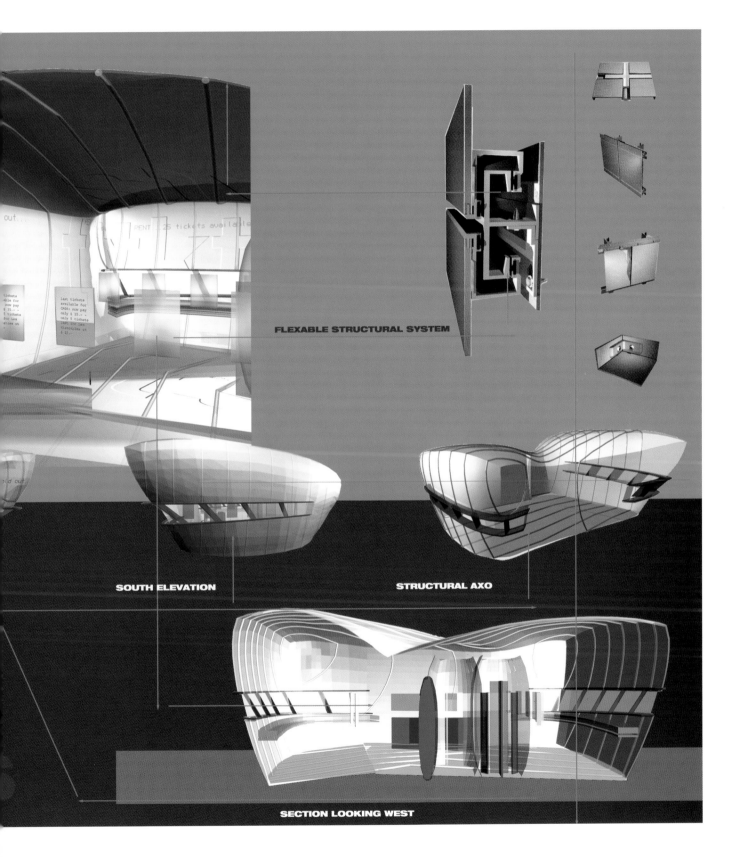

FLEXABLE STRUCTURAL SYSTEM

SOUTH ELEVATION

STRUCTURAL AXO

SECTION LOOKING WEST

ARCHI-**TECTONICS**

3

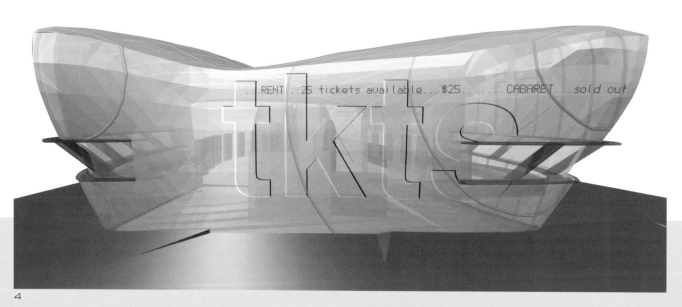

4

3   Perspective of 'soft booth' in Times
     Square

4   Elevation with integral texts

5   Three-dimensional horizontal section
     cut; top view of interior

6   Inflated volume of booth with program

CYBER**SPACE**

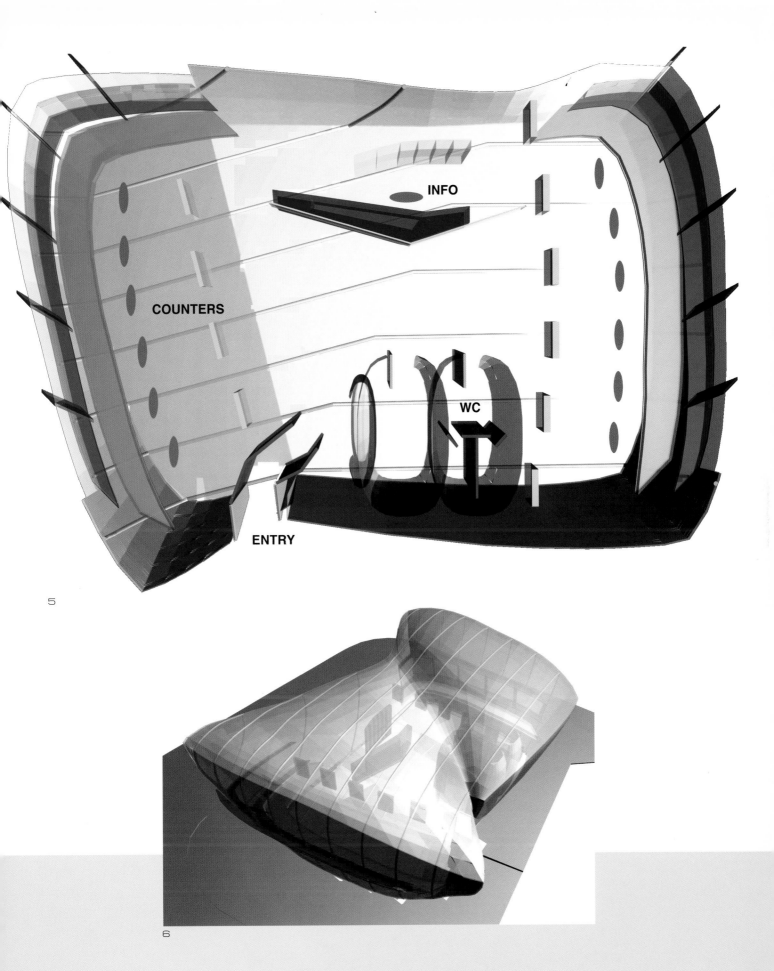

INFO

COUNTERS

WC

ENTRY

5

6

KMD ARCHITECTS

TOWER OF 120 STORIES

Recent advances in structural engineering and constructability, combined with the ability to design directly with the computer, have made new forms possible. These forms can follow the fluidity of nature. Nature has always been seen as universally beautiful and as possessing inherent integrity, balance, and proportion. Humans have, in the past, designed in opposition to nature; however, the 21st century will embrace nature in very high-tech ways. The shapes of this century will express natural forms like the blade of grass or the strength of the wind. This design for a very tall building expresses the fluidity and transient basis of 21st-century life: a fleeting moment, a temporal gesture.

1-4 Exterior view

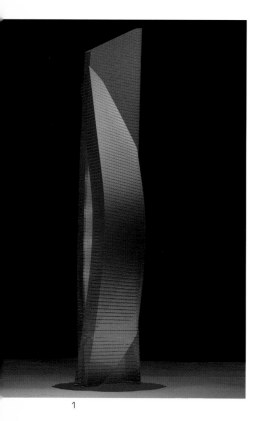

1

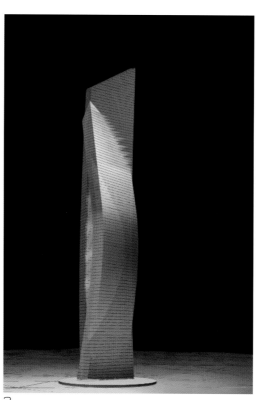

2

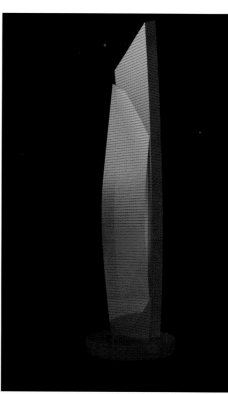

3

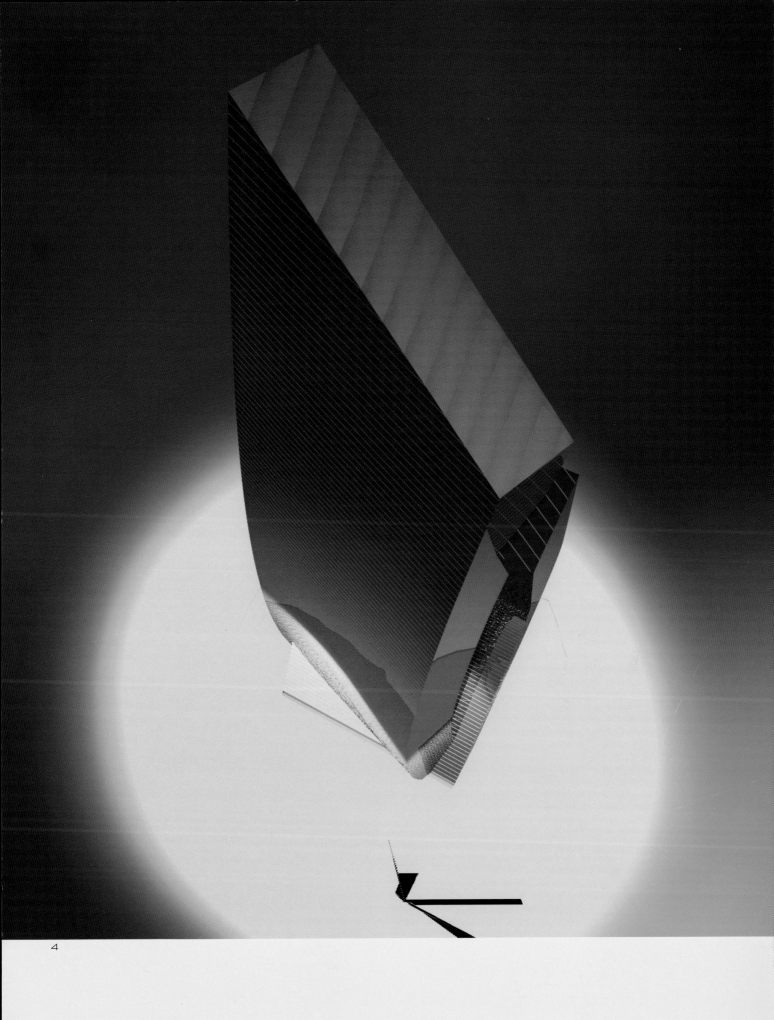

OOSTERHUIS.NL

Trans-ports is a distributed network that facilitates and structures communication between real and virtual people to suit real and virtual environments. The three-dimensional, real-time evolution game resides in the Trans-ports network, generating a meta-language in the real-time evolving form and content of the deformable multi-user, multisensory environments.

The Trans-ports network, connecting local populations of users in real-time to a distributed global population of users, includes augmented real and virtual shared environments, where novices and professionals explore educational and commercial interactions between real people, real building bodies, and their virtual avatar-counterparts.

The evolving information content, that is seamlessly integrated into the interior and/or exterior skins of the transforming real and virtual demonstrators, is broadcasted on a timesharing basis by both non-profit and commercial

organizations. The instrumental building bodies are feeding on the redundant meta-language information flow of the real-time evolution game; as a result their information contents are evolving in a process of continuous transformation.

1&2   A flexible rubber skin exterior covers the hydraulic spaceframe structure; it fluently follows displacements in the shape

3   The real-time evolution game generates data and this changes the shape of Trans-ports

1

2

3

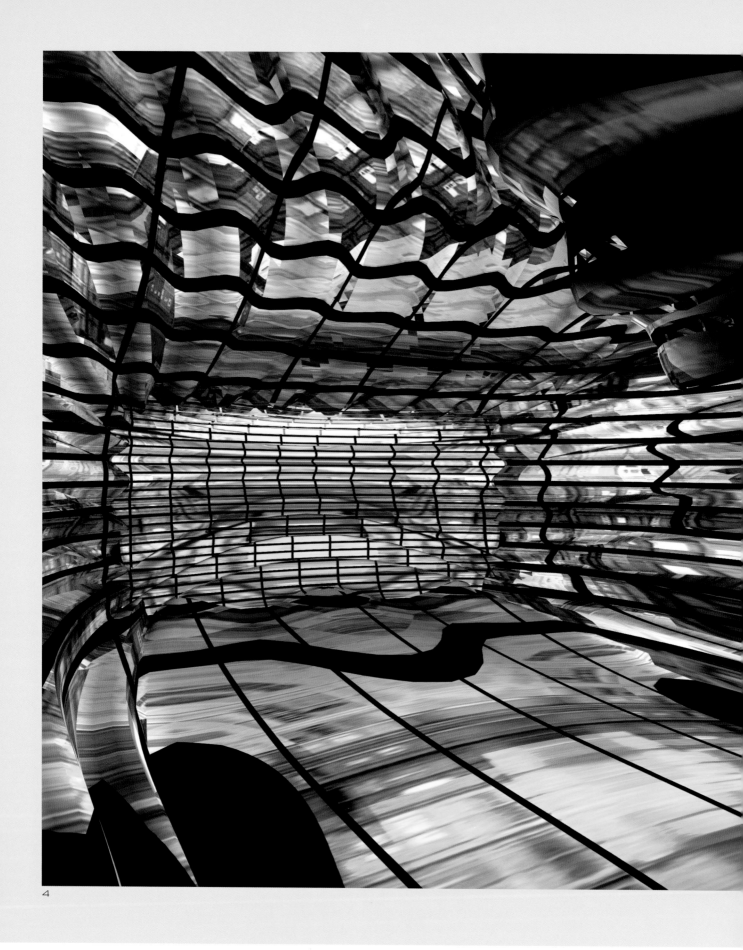

4

5

6

4&6 The real-time evolution game
      generates data and this changes the
      shape of Trans-ports

  5 Flexible electronic interior skin; it
      displays text and images in real-time

MARY LOU MAHER, UNIVERSITY OF SYDNEY

VIRTUAL CONFERENCE FACILITIES

The Virtual Conference Facilities design is part of the Virtual Campus, which comprises several rooms, hallways, and resource areas. The rooms include facilities for slide projection, recording, and softbots. The three-dimensional visualization of the rooms assumes that an avatar can walk or teleport from one place to another. The design style is a derivation of the Virtual Office design, using similar frame-like walls and distinctive activity areas.

The facility has three main rooms: the entrance hall, the conference room, and the practice studio. The use of rooms is determined on the basis of activity and conversation privacy, since the main purpose of the facility is to provide a place for people to meet. A person can hear anyone else in the same room talk but cannot hear someone in another room.

1   Main hall is entrance to entire Virtual Campus, one of the frames being entrance to conference room. Receptionist is a conversational robot (or softbot)

2   Conference room has two portals, one at each end; one portal leads to main hall and the other to practice studio

3   Each portal is an animated rotating door

4   Conference room has curved frame-like walls that display information about presentations and discussions

1

2

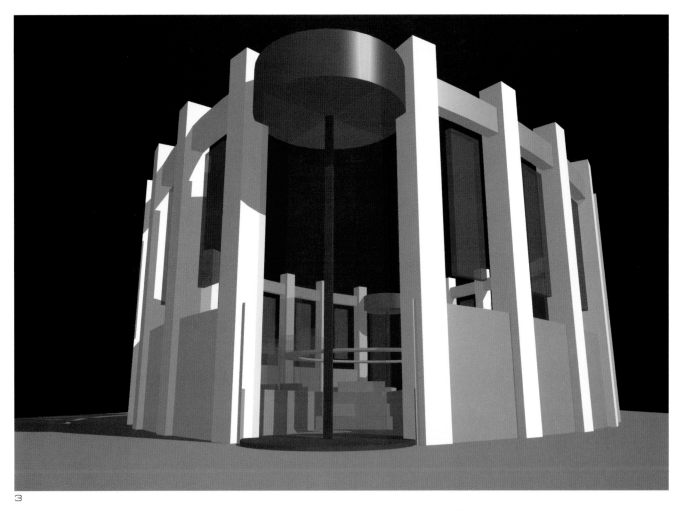

3

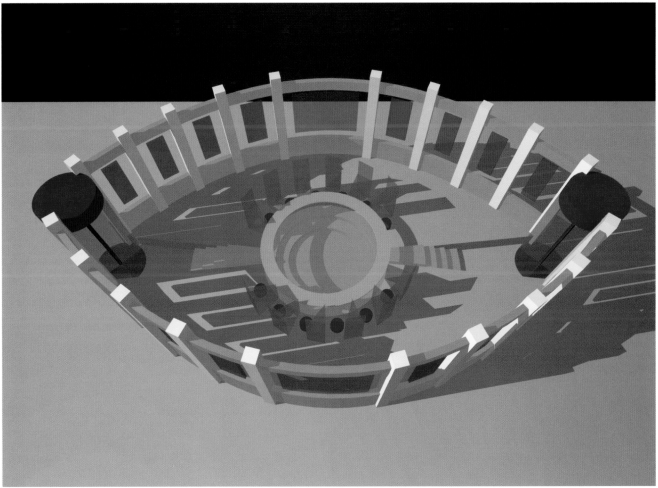

4

MARY LOU MAHER, **UNIVERSITY OF SYDNEY**

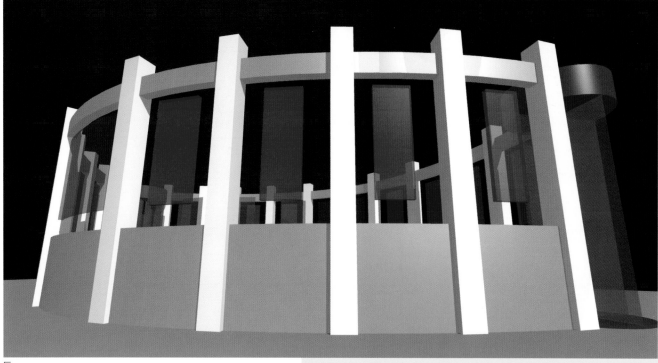

5

6

5 Walls in conference room provide access to presentations, papers, discussions, and notices

6 Stairs lead from portal to floating ring to create virtual movement

7 Practice studio is a quiet room for participants to prepare presentations using the virtual slide projector

8 Each person has a separate place indicated by a disk on the floor and a glass panel

9 Cubes forming walls of practice studio represent virtual tools

10 Conference attendees stand around a floating ring to focus discussion and presentation views

CYBER**SPACE**

7

8

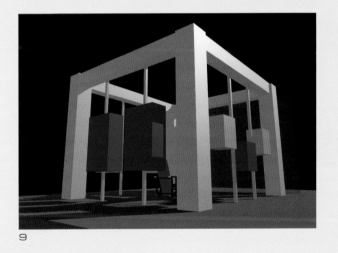

9

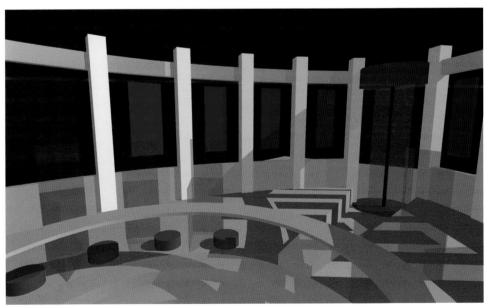

10

MARY LOU MAHER, UNIVERSITY OF SYDNEY

A VIRTUAL OFFICE

The Virtual Office design provides an environment in a three-dimensional virtual world in which a person, as an avatar, works alone or holds meetings with others. Two aspects of the design emphasize the 'virtual': the walls and the allocation of areas. The design assumes that the walls of a virtual office provide a visual boundary to the place that indicates what is inside and what is outside the office. The functions of the walls include security, privacy, and a place for hanging things. The three-dimensional visualization of the wall as a frame with cubes was inspired by the paintings of Piet Mondriaan. The design has five functional areas that are distinct in location, in order to provide a sense of movement when moving from one type of task to another.

1

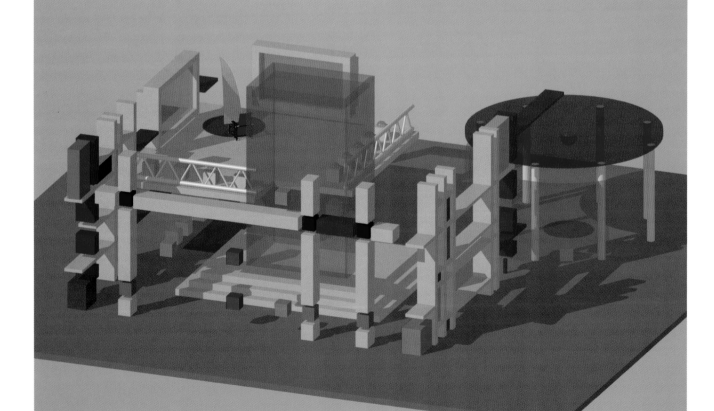

2

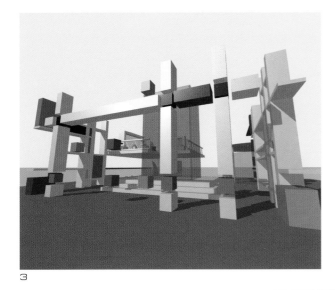

3

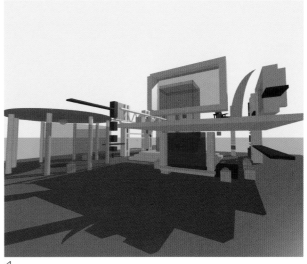

4

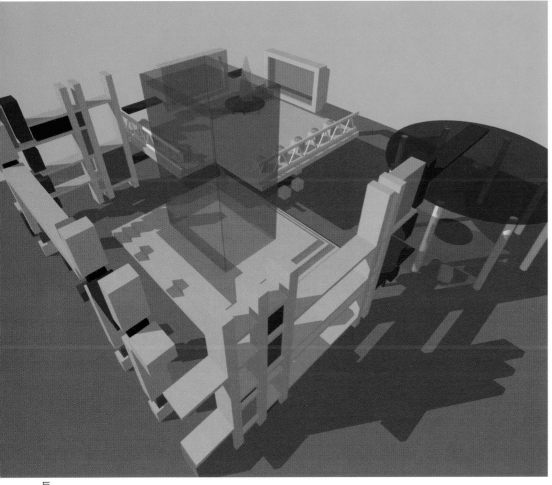

5

1 Entrance provides an introduction to
virtual office, as well as security and
messaging devices

2 Cylindrical entrance area and rectangular
prism enclose all other areas

3 Cubes on walls representing different
functions can be relocated

4 Screens provide an equivalent to the
computer monitor, and feature as the
place for information outside the office

5 Frame-like walls provide security and
privacy through software

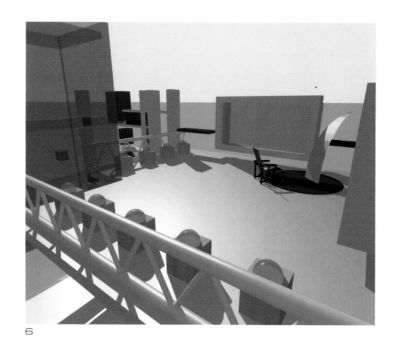

6

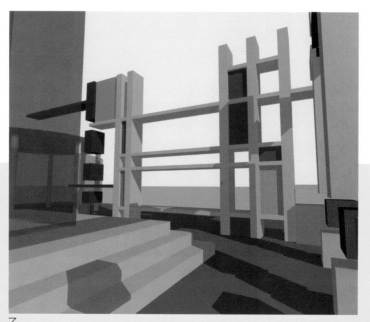

7

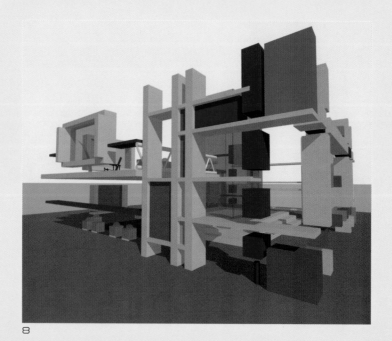

8

CYBER**SPACE**

6 Working area provides a range of office tools, with a chair to symbolize that a person is there

7 Communication area is for meeting and working collaboratively; stairs provide informal seating

8 Mondriaan's paintings inspired placement of frames

9 Lift moves avatar from one level to another, symbolizing a change in activity

10 Relaxation area provides access to online entertainment

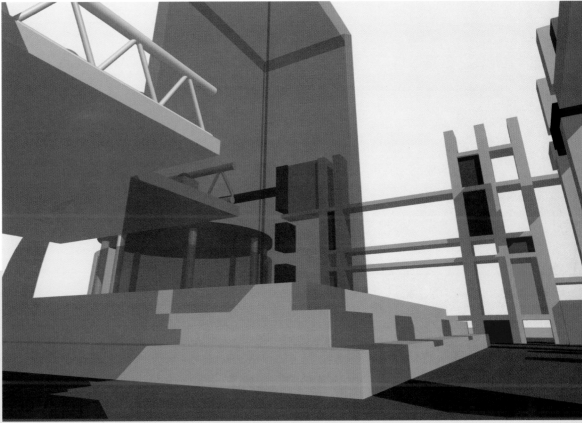

9

10

WAVEKNOT

In Waveknot, the columnar morphology (see pages 38–9) is transformed into an undulated architectural surface defined by a simple knot space. Within a possible architectural setting, the space can be a transitional one, linking two primary spaces as it winds from one to another. In another setting, the space itself can be a primary one suited for linear layouts dealing with spatial or temporal sequencing of functions or events.

The surface can be constructed from modules, and employs new building technology, from both structural morphologic and software-driven manufacturing standpoints. In the rendition shown here, opaque modules constructed from rippled corrugated metal are combined with transparent rippled corrugations in glass or plastic.

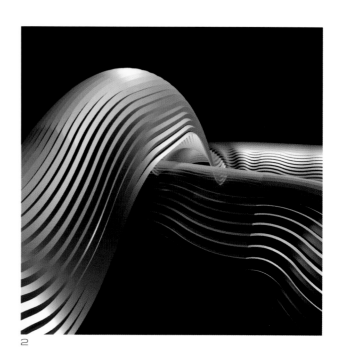

2

1

3

4

REISER & UMEMOTO

WEST SIDE CONVERGENCE

Design Intent

Cities are the nexus of material and information flows, developed within multiple infrastructures of transportation, distribution, culture, and knowledge. The increasingly interconnected world has produced cities where global systems are intermeshed in local environments, and scale shifts rapidly from the local to the regional and international. As the locus of intense economic, social, and idea exchanges and connections at all levels, the city of the 21st century must support these vital urban interactions, and design new meeting, working, and entertainment environments.

The opportunity came to reinvent this site by transcending the separation and monofunctionality of many of its large infrastructural elements through a mode of operation that the firm terms 'infrastructuralism.' There are very real benefits—social and political as well as functional and economic—to the loosening of the stratification of infrastructure and activity in this area.

Since the 19th century, infrastructure has been overtly utilized as a model resulting in the amplification of systems of movement, distribution, and control. While the proliferation of these systems has necessarily been attendant to modernization, they are rarely questioned or seen as anything other than discrete components of a hierarchy no greater than its parts. Reflexively, the after-effect of such thinking has been the intensely stratified conception of the city and how its systems relate to one another. In this sense the site in question is astonishingly paradigmatic of this phenomenon, with the profound separation and ensuing monofunctionality of each of its singular (albeit colossal) programs.

Even developers shy away from this area, seeing its radical segmentation (in both time and space) as an insurmountable obstacle to the kind of urban activity that would justify a return on their investment. And while the city has always been an engine for the flow of capital, this is not its only reason for being. It is thus at the level of the urban substrate that the project operates to produce change in the form of the city. Working in this mode constitutes an alternative to master planning, not as a negative critique, but rather as an affirmative departure.

1   Section through Jacob Javits Center
    Exhibition level extension

2   Exploded isometric of project

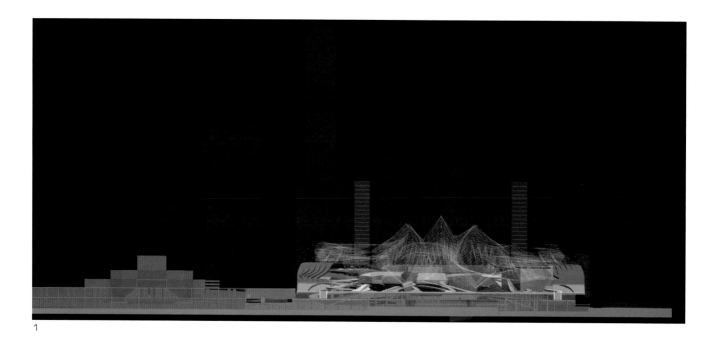

1

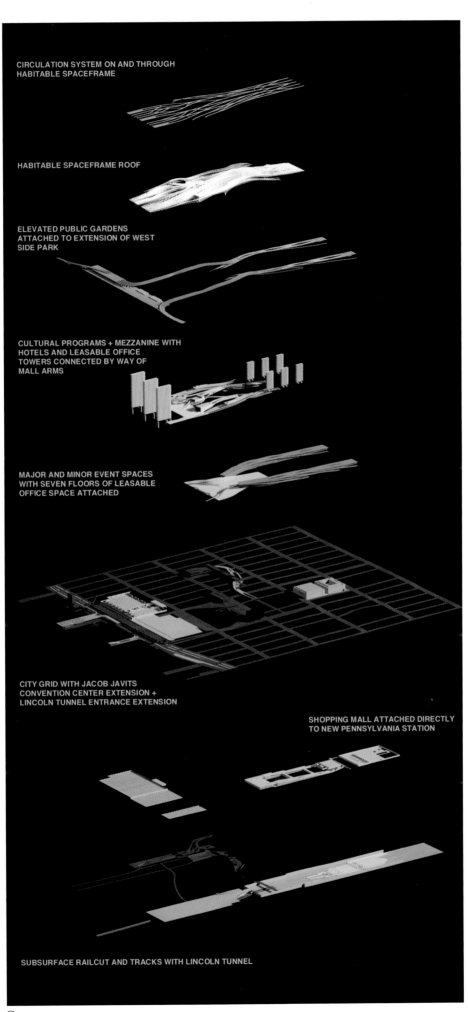

CIRCULATION SYSTEM ON AND THROUGH
HABITABLE SPACEFRAME

HABITABLE SPACEFRAME ROOF

ELEVATED PUBLIC GARDENS
ATTACHED TO EXTENSION OF WEST
SIDE PARK

CULTURAL PROGRAMS + MEZZANINE WITH
HOTELS AND LEASABLE OFFICE
TOWERS CONNECTED BY WAY OF
MALL ARMS

MAJOR AND MINOR EVENT SPACES
WITH SEVEN FLOORS OF LEASABLE
OFFICE SPACE ATTACHED

CITY GRID WITH JACOB JAVITS
CONVENTION CENTER EXTENSION +
LINCOLN TUNNEL ENTRANCE EXTENSION

SHOPPING MALL ATTACHED DIRECTLY
TO NEW PENNSYLVANIA STATION

SUBSURFACE RAILCUT AND TRACKS WITH LINCOLN TUNNEL

3

4

5

3 View inside habitable roof of event space and Spaceframe parkspace offering varied environments

4 Detail of cultural programming in roof

5 Bird's-eye view of proposal looking east from above Hudson River

6 Relationship of proposal to Midtown

7 Detail of habitable roof landscape

8 View looking west towards the Hudson River; extension of Hudson River Park meets habitable roof landscape

6

7

8

Aegis Hypo-Surface
Credit: dECOi
dECOi: Mark Goulthorpe, Oliver Dering, Arnaud Descombes and Gabriel Evangelisti; with David Glover, Ove Arup and Partners (engineering); Dr Alex Scott & Professor Keith Ball (mathematics); Keith Wood & Xavier Robitaille (programming); and Professor Mark Burry & Grant Dunlop, Deakin University (modeling/programming)

AIDA Hairsalon
New York, New York, USA
Archi-tectonics
Principal Architect: Winka Dubbeldam
Project Team: Ty Tikari, Nicola Bauman, Patricia Herniaz-Driever

Architecture Faculty, University of Venice
Venice, Italy
Digit-all Studio
Credit: Ammar Eloueini, Digit-all Studio with R, DSV & Sie P

Architecture Faculty, University of Venice
Venice, Italy
UN Studio van Berkel & Bos
Design: Ben van Berkel in collaboration with Cecil Belmond (Ove Arup & Partners)
Design Team: Hans Sterck, Remco Bruggink, Laura Negrini, Sonja Cabalt (graphic design), Paul Vriend, Yuri Werner
Consultants: Ludo Grooteman, Caroline Bos, Tobias Wallisser.
Technical Advisor: Ove Arup & Partners, London

The Boolean House
Grant Dunlop & Mark Burry, Deakin University, Australia
Credit: All modeling and rendering by Grant Dunlop
The Captor
A project by Christopher Romero
Email address: chris@oscillation.com
Produced by Oscillation/Studio 313
Project Team: Christopher Romero assisted by Winston Yang

Chimerical Housings: Mass Customized Housing
Credit: Kolatan/Mac Donald Studio
Design Team: Sulan Kolatan and William Mac Donald, Principals; with S. Colombo and D. Desimone (project coordinators); L. Malibran, Y. do Campo, C. D. Brunn, J. Sanchez, R. Hom, E. Bourlier, M. Small, M. McNamara, J. Malley, J. Baker, A. Olsen
Acknowledgements: Alisa/Wavefront

The Cine Experimental Film Center
Brooklyn, New York, USA
Project Team: Hariri & Hariri; Gisue Hariri, Mojgan Hariri, Anne Uhlmann, Marc Stierlin, Nadya Liebich
Consultants: Texas Instruments

Cloud Cover
Dr Haresh Lalvani
Computer Modeling: Neil Katz
Computer Rendering: Mohamad Al-Khayer

Column Museum
Dr Haresh Lalvani
Computer Modeling: Neil Katz
Computer Rendering: Mohamad Al-Khayer
Prototype Development: Bruce Gitlin and Alex Kveton, Milgo/Bufkin

Cultural Information Exchange Center
New York, New York, USA
Digit-all Studio
Credit: Ammar Eloueini and Céline Parmentier

Cyberport
Telegraph Bay, Hong Kong SAR
Arquitectonica (ARQ) International
All images are courtesy of the Government of Hong Kong Special Administrative Region.
Partners-in-Charge of Design: Bernardo Fort Brescia FAIA, Laurinda Spear FAIA
Project Director: Chris Reynolds
Project Manager: Jacqueline Gonzalez, Stuart Berriman
Project Team: Shawn Bruins, Arturo Griego, John Jenkins, William Lai, Quenifer Lee, Todd Martin, Julio Mendez, Matthew McCallum, Robin Romero and Jorge Salcedo
Renderings (Digital): Digitart for Arquitectonica (ARQ) and KO Lab/Max Strang Studio for Arquitectonica (ARQ)
Renderings (Pastel): Jim Piatt for Arquitectonica (ARQ)
Architect of Record: Wong Tung & Partners Limited
Associate Architects: The Jerde Partnership
Consultants
Planning Consultant: City Planning Consultants Ltd.
Landscaping Consultant: Belt Collins Hong Kong Ltd.
Structural Consultant: Maunsell Structural Consultants Ltd.
Mechanical Engineering Consultant: Ove Arup & Partners Hong Kong Limited
Traffic Consultant: Maunsell Consultants Asia Ltd.
Environmental Consultant: Maunsell Environment Management Consultants Ltd.
Management Consultant: Crow Maunsell Management Consultants
Quantity Surveyor: Levett & Bailey Chartered Quantity Surveyors Limited
Façade Consultant: Arup Façade Engineering
Fire Engineering Consultant: Arup Fire
IT Consultant: Arup Communications, The Broadcast Design Group Limited
Lighting Consultant: Doublevision (joint venture L'Observatoire International/Linbeck & Rausch)

Digital Design Process, Arch 135
UC Berkeley Students
Course: Architecture 135, Process and Methods of Modeling and Presentation
Instructor: John Marx AIA, Lecturer, UC Berkeley, Design Principal Form4 Architects
Students: Elisa Lui, Jerry Jai, Wilson Au-Yeung, Vivien Tso, William Hsien

The Digital House
Hariri & Hariri
Architect: Hariri & Hariri (Gisue Hariri & Mojgan Hariri, Principals)
Design Team: Gisue Hariri, Mojgan Hariri, Karin Mousson
Walk-through Animation: Proun Space Studio (John Bennett & Gustavo Bonevardi)
Animation Narration & Voice: John Brehm
Model Maker: Nadya Liebich and Marla Pasareno
LCD Technology Engineer: Mark Borstelmann, LCD Planar Optics

Dis-a—Pier Fluid Topologies
Yokohama, Japan
Archi-tectonics
Credit: Winka Dubbeldam, Archi-tectonics; with Maggie Mahboubian

Ephemeral Urban Fields
Studio 8 Architects
Credit: C.J. Lim, Lee Harris, Matt Springett + Ed Liu

Federation Square
Melbourne, Australia
Credit: Lab + Bates Smart Architects
Rendering: Gollings + Pidgeon, Lab + Bates Smart Architects and Lab architecture studio

Floriade NH Pavilion
Haarlemmermeer, The Netherlands
Oosterhuis.nl
Project Architect: Kas Oosterhuis
Design Team: Kas Oosterhuis, Ilona Lénárd, Andre Houdart, Marc Benerink, Birte Steffan, Franziska Groening, Stephanie Buenau, Giorgio Martocchia
Film: Kroon & Wissenraet, Amsterdam
Three-dimensional models/renderings/drawings by Oosterhuis.nl

Future Generations University
Credit: Lab architecture studio

Gateshead Theatre
Credit: dECOi for Foster & Partners
dECOi: Mark Goulthorpe, Arnaud Descombes, Gaspard Giroud with Dr Alex Scott UCL (mathematics)

Goteborg: The Museum of Global Culture 1998
Archi-tectonics
Credit: Winka Dubbeldam, Archi-tectonics

Ground Zero I
Santa Monica, California, USA
Credit: Shubin + Donaldson
Photo Credit: Tom Bonner (1)

Ground Zero II
Santa Monica, California, USA
Credit: Shubin + Donaldson

Guggenheim Virtual Museum
Credit: Asymptote Architecture

Helsinki Music Center
Helsinki, Finland
Oosterhuis.nl
Project Architect: Kas Oosterhuis
Design Team: Kas Oosterhuis, Ilona Lénárd, Andre Houdart, Marc Benerink, Giorgio Martocchia, Franziska Groening, Stephanie Buenau
Renderings/drawings/models: Oosterhuis.nl

HyperHouse
Crowd Productions
Project Concept: Michael Trudgeon, Anthony Kitchener
Project Design: Michael Trudgeon
Computer Rendering: Glynis Teo

Idea Cloud
Tristan d'Estree Sterk & Robert Woodbury
Authors: Tristan d'Estree Sterk & Robert Woodbury
Architect: Tristan d'Estree Sterk, School of Architecture, Landscape Architecture and Urban Design, Adelaide University

Institute for Electronic Clothing
HyperSurface Systems, Inc.
Credits: Stephen Perrella, Kunio Kudo and Tony Wong

The Moebius House Study
HyperSurface Systems, Inc.
Credits: Stephen Perrella, Rebecca Carpenter, 1998

Munich Airport, Terminal 2, Competition Entry
Credit: Kohn Pedersen Fox Associates (London)

Music Theatre, Graz 1998–2003
Graz, Steiermark, Austria
UN Studio van Berkel & Bos
Design: Ben van Berkel (UN Studio) in collaboration with Cecil Balmond (Ove Arup & Partners, London)
Design Phase
Project Team: Hannes Pfau (project co-ordinator), Peter Trummer (design co-ordinator), Markus Berger
Collaborators: Maarten van Tuijl. Karel Deckers, Do Janne Vermeulen
Competition Phase
Design Team: Ben van Berkel, Susanne Boyer, Remco Bruggink, Pedro Campos Costa, Ludo Grooteman, KSK Tamura
Project Team: Sonja Cabalt (graphic design), Marco Jongmans (model), Jeroen Kreijne (model), Marc Prins, Armin Hess
Collaborators: Eli Aschkenasy, Andreas Bogenschütz, Caroline Bos, Walther Kloet, Hannes Pfau, Thomas Schonder, Henri Snel, Peter Trummer, Jacco van Wengerden, Tobias Wallisser, Mark Westerhuis

National Museum of Contemporary Art 1996–2002
Osaka, Japan
Cesar Pelli & Associates Inc
Credits: M Lafoe/CP&A (1); G. Bekerman/CP&A (2–5); Sight Corp & Field Jam (6)

Observatorium for a Polder
New York, New York, USA
Kolatan/Mac Donald Studio
Design Team: Ayse Sulan Kolatan and William Mac Donald, Principals; with Stephano Colombo, Yolanda do Campo, Christian Bruun, Maia Small, and Linda Malibran
Acknowledgements: Alias/Wavefront

Ocean Membrane
Shoreline Membrane Design Competition 1999
Credit: Ocean UK Team—Frank Harding, Alex Thompson, Tom Verebes

Ogilvy & Mather Advertising Agency
Culver City, Los Angeles, USA
Credit: Shubin + Donaldson

Operation [Interface]
Ocean UK and Ocean US
Ocean UK: Tom Verebes, Director; Anne Laure Gimenez, Director; Architecte DPLG, IFA, Thomas Knuvener
Ocean US: Robert Elfer, Director, AIA, OAQ and Wade Stevens, Director

Paramorph I
Mark Burry & Grant Dunlop
Credit: Professor Mark Burry and Grant Dunlop, School of Architecture and Building, Deakin University, Australia

Paramorph II
South Bank, London, England
dECOi Architect(e)s/Deakin University
dECOi Architect(e)s, Paris, France: Mark Goulthorpe, Gabrielle Evangelisti, Gaspard Giroud, Felix Robbins, Franck Deschaux
School of Architecture and Building, Deakin University, Australia: Professor Mark Burry, Grant Dunlop, Andrew Maher
Ove Arup & Partners (Structural Engineers), London, England; David Glover and E. Clark

Raybould House and Garden
Kolatan/Mac Donald Studio
Design Team: Sulan Kolatan and William Mac Donald, Principals; with Erich Schoenenberger and Jonathan Baker
Consultants: Andre Chaszar and Angus Palmer of Buro Happold Engineers

Resi-Rise Skyscraper
New York, New York. USA
Kolatan/Mac Donald Studio
Design Team: Sulan Kolatan and William Mac Donald, Principals; S. Colombo and J. Baker, (project coordinators); L. Malibran, Y. do Campo, G. Rojas, C.D. Bruun, A. Burk, B. Schenk, and M. Kosmidou
Consultants: Andre Chaszar of Buro Happold Engineers

Salt Water Pavilion
Neeltje Jans, The Netherlands
Oosterhuis.nl
Design: Oosterhuis.nl
Project Architect: Kas Oosterhuis
Design Team: Kas Oosterhuis, Ilona Lénárd, Menno Rubbens
Design Hydra: Ilona Lénárd, Visual Artist
Design Light Environment: Kas Oosterhuis
Programming Lights: Menno Rubbens, Arjen van der Schoot, Fairlight
Design Virtual Worlds: Kas Oosterhuis
Realization VR: Marino Gouwens, Eline Wieland, Károly Tóth, Green Dino
Sound Environment: Edwin van der Heide, Victor Wentinck
Sensors: Bert Bongers
Photographs/renderings/drawings: Oosterhuis.nl

Sarajevo Concert Hall
Sarajevo, Bosnia-Herzegovina
Digit-all Studio
Credit: Ammar Eloueini, Céline Parmentier, Nathalie Roubaut, Nikola Jankovic

Silopera
Rotterdam, The Netherlands
Credit: Alsop & Störmer

Sound Studio
Credit: Shubin + Donaldson

Spheroids
Dr Haresh Lalvani
Computer Modeling: Neil Katz
Computer Rendering: Mohamad Al Khayer

Strategic (Re)Occupations
Governors Island, New York, USA
Archi-tectonics
Principal Architect: Winka Dubbeldam
Project Team: Phillip Mohr, Ivo Nelissen, Julie Shurtz

Sunlaw Power Plant Canopy & Enclosure
Los Angeles, California, USA
Moore Ruble Yudell, Architects & Planners
Project Credits
Owner: Sunlaw Energy Corporation
Chairman: Robert N. Danziger
President: Michael A. Levin
Project Manager: Timothy G. Smith
Design Architect: Moore Ruble Yudell
Principal-in-Charge, Principal Architect: John Ruble
Principal Architect: Buzz Yudell
Associate-in-Charge/Project Architect: James Mary O'Connor
Project Team: Ross Morishige, Lisa Belian
Digital Renderings: Ross Morishige
Color and Materials: Tina Beebe
Graphic Design: Janet Sager

Temporal Civic Zone
Credit: Dr Michael J. Ostwald, University of Newcastle, Australia

Theater de Warande
Turnhout, Belgium
Oosterhuis.nl
Design: Oosterhuis.nl
Project Architect: Kas Oosterhuis
Design Team: Kas Oosterhuis, Andre Houdart, Marc Benerink
Building Costs Advisor: Bureau Bouwkunde, Antwerp
Three-dimensional models/renderings/drawings: Oosterhuis.nl

Times Square Discount Ticketing Center
New York, New York, USA
Ocean UK and Ocean US
Ocean UK: Tom Verebes, Director
Ocean US: Robert Elfer, Director, AIA, OAQ; Wade Stevens, Director; Gus Wendell, Rich Wrightson, Kevin Cespedes

TKTS—Booth at Times Square
New York, New York, USA
Archi-tectonics
Principal Architect: Winka Dubbeldam
Assistant: Kenny Endo

Tower of 120 Stories
120 Story Office Tower Competition
Seoul, Korea
Architect: Kaplan McLaughlin Diaz (KMD) Architects, San Francisco, California
Design Director: Herbert McLaughlin
Project Designer: John Marx
Rendering: Andrew Wong

Trans-ports
Oosterhuis.nl
Project Management: Kas Oosterhuis, Ole Bouman
Design: Oosterhuis.nl
Design Team: Kas Oosterhuis, Andre Houdart
Three-dimensional models/renderings: Oosterhuis.nl

Virtual Conference Facilities
Mary Lou Maher, University of Sydney, Australia
Credit: Dr Mary Lou Maher, Professor Design Computing; Dr Simeon Simoff, Research Fellow; Mr Ning Gu, Research Assistant and Mr Kok Hong Lau, Research Assistant.

A Virtual Office
Mary Lou Maher, University of Sydney, Australia
Credit: Dr Mary Lou Maher, Professor Design Computing; Dr Simeon Simoff, Research Fellow; Mr Ning Gu, Research Assistant and Mr Kok Hong Lau, Research Assistant.

Waveknot
Dr Haresh Lalvani
Computer Modeling: Mohamad Al-Khayer and Neil Katz
Computer Rendering: Mohamad Al-Khayer
Prototype Development: Bruce Gitlin and Alex Kveton, Milgo/Bufkin

West Side Convergence
New York, New York, USA
Reiser + Umemoto, Rur Architecture P.C.
Consulting Engineers: Ysrael A. Seinuk P.C.
Planning and Transportation Consultants: Buckhurst Fish & Jacquemart
Principals: Jesse Reiser + Nanako Umemoto
Design Team: Jason Payne, Yama Karim, Nona Yehia and David Ruy
Assistants: Wolfgang Gollwitzer, Astrid Phiber and Matthias Blass
Interns: Keisuke Kitagawa, Ade Herkarisma and Joseph Chang

Avatar: a graphical icon that represents a real person in a cyberspace system. When you enter the system, you can choose from a number of fanciful avatars. Sophisticated three-dimensional avatars even change shape depending on what they are doing (for example, walking or sitting).

Chromakey: electronically matting or inserting an image from one camera into the picture produced by another, also called 'keying'. The subject to be inserted is shot against a solid color background (blue screen), signals from the two sources are merged through a special effects generator.

Datascape: fields of information, or entities inherent with distributive data.

Elastomer: any of various elastic materials that resemble rubber (that is, resumes its original shape when a deforming force is removed).

Euclidean: based on the geometric postulates first described by the Greek geometer Euclid (c300 BC). This is the straight-line and flat-plane geometry we are familiar with, a geometry where parallel lines never meet and where the sum of angles in a triangle equal 180 degrees.

Hyper: 'over' or 'above' the normal.

Hyperculture: a culture characterized by an excessive or exaggerated level of complexity of information, experiences, choices and possibilities.

Hyperflexible space: space that can be reconfigured dramatically both formally and aesthetically and continuously. A space where such characteristics are fundamentally inherent.

Hypergeometry: higher dimensional geometry, that is, the geometry of spaces and structures beyond the familiar three dimensions of space.

Hyperization: the process of making something 'over' or 'above' the normal; extension into the 'hyper' stage or state.

Hyperspace: higher dimensional space, that is, space having more than the familiar three dimensions of space.

Hypersurface: a higher dimensional surface, that is, a surface defined by more than three dimensions of space.

Hyperuniverse: in the context here, it is meant as a meta-universe, that is, a conceptual universe underlying the physical universe, having a higher dimensional geometry.

Meta-architecture: architecture based on the manipulation of morphologically structured information.

Metalanguage: a language or vocabulary used to describe, analyze or define another language.

Moebius strip: a continuous one-sided surface that can be formed from a rectangular strip by rotating one end 180° and attaching it to the other end.

Morphogenetics: the science of morphogenesis, the origin and development of form; the study dealing with the genetic code of form or the genetic basis of form.

Morphology: study of form (Greek *morphe*, form); the study of the principles of form, structure and pattern across and within disciplines.

Mechanical Vapor Recompression (MVR): an industrial process whereby water is boiled in a vacuum, requiring less energy to distil.

Oblate: shortened or shrunk along an axis.

Pedagogical: of, relating to, or befitting a teacher or education; an approach to teaching that encompasses various techniques of abstraction, precedent and experiments.

Photovoltaic: capable of producing a voltage when exposed to radiant energy, especially light.

Prolate: elongated or stretched along an axis.

Robocolor: a popular and reliable intelligent color changing spotlight that has served the lighting industry for years the world over.

Sensorium: the entire sensory system of a building-body. The place where external impressions are localized, and transformed into sensations, prior to being reflected to other parts of the organism.

Spaceframe: a three-dimensional assemblage of beams forming a rigid structure (such as a roof truss).

Spatial: of or pertaining to space; occurring in space, or having extension in space.

Tabula Rasa: an absence of presupposition and incorporation for infinite possibilities.

Temporal: of or pertaining to time; occurring in time, or having extension in time.

Unibody: the result of a manufacturing process where sheet metal body parts are combined (welded together) with stress-bearing elements to form the body and chassis as a single piece, as opposed to attaching body parts to a frame.

INDEX & ACKNOWLEDGMENTS

IMAGES is pleased to present *Cyberspace: The World of Digital Architecture* to its compendium of design and architectural publications.
We wish to thank all participating individuals and firms for their valuable contributions and a special thanks to Maggie Toy for her inspiration with the concept and title of this publication.